An American Paradox

AN AMERICAN PARADOX

Censorship in a Nation
of Free Speech

PATRICK GARRY

Westport, Connecticut
London

Library of Congress Cataloging-in-Publication Data

Garry, Patrick M.
    An American paradox : censorship in a nation of free speech / Patrick
Garry.
        p.   cm.
    ISBN 0-275-94522-7 (alk. paper)
    1. Censorship – United States.   I. Title.
Z658.U5G37   1993
363.3′1 – dc20   92-31846

British Library Cataloguing in Publication Data is available.

Library of Congress Catalog Card Number: 92-31846
ISBN: 0-275-94522-7

First published in 1993

Praeger Publishers, 88 Post Road West, Westport, Connecticut 06881
An imprint of Greenwood Publishing Group, Inc.

Printed in the United States of America

∞™

The paper used in this book complies with the
Permanent Paper Standard issued by the National
Information Standards Organization (Z39.48–1984).

10 9 8 7 6 5 4 3 2 1

For Elizabeth

Contents

Contradictions abound in human life. In American society, one of the most enduring contradictions has involved censorship in a nation devoted to speech. Despite the lessons of history, censorship continues to flourish in the arts, music, television, advertising, and even in the university. Indeed, of all the struggles waged in the 1960s, perhaps the one thought victorious was that against censorship. Yet as adults, the generation of the 1960s is sponsoring a campaign of censorship more widespread than the one they faced as youths. The reasons for this censorship crusade may reveal much about the character of American society.

The opponents of censorship have traditionally argued that it emanates from the intolerant and repressive strains in society. Yet America is probably the most free and tolerant nation on earth. Moreover, as is especially the case now, the advocates of freedom on some issues have ended up as the promoters of censorship on others.

Thus, censorship becomes merely the throwing out of all the unnecessary clutter of speech; it acts like the street-cleaner of the public dialogue. Perhaps the increasing occurrence of censorship suggests that modern society would rather have a little silence than a lot of noise.

The erosion and weakening of modern communities have spawned many social problems, such as the escalation of crime and the decline of public education and child safety. Free speech advocates have often believed that censorship thrives in strong or tight-knit communities. This chapter argues the opposite: Censorship occurs in communities that are weak and unstable. Thus, the breakdown of community may now even be threatening individual liberty.

Though America is often seen as an optimistic and even overconfident nation, it does have its insecure and anxious side. When this side of the national psyche is exposed, its symptoms include censorship. The current phase of cultural censorship suggests an America insecure over the health and future of its social fabric.

Acknowledgments

My fellowship at the Freedom Forum Media Studies Center at Columbia University provided the time, resources, and inspiration to write this book. I am immensely grateful to Ev Dennis and his talented staff for their generous support and capable assistance. Special thanks must go to Beth Hoffman and Lisa DeLisle for their editorial contributions, and to Wendy Boyd for her technical assistance. And as always, I am grateful to Paul Murphy for his valuable insights into the enigmatic realm of speech and censorship in America.

Introduction

Understanding American society has been a preoccupation since the British government tried to figure out how to govern and control its independent-minded colonies. This task has been complicated by the constantly changing nature of American society. In less than a century and a half, it has evolved from a nation where the Irish were the most recent and the most unwanted immigrants, where women could not vote, and where the Mason-Dixon line divided two radically different cultures within a single nation. Moreover, the country will continue to change in the future: By the year 2001, whites will be in the minority in America.

The task of understanding America has been made ever more difficult by this country's democratic character. Democracies are more fluid and changing than are other more hierarchical and homogeneous societies. Yet because of this democratic nature, the need to understand the national character and identity takes on greater urgency. Indeed, the self-governance of a nation requires an understanding of that nation. And like any kind of knowledge, human and social understanding comes through communication.

Although the United States is unquestionably a nation of speakers and of incessant communication, it is also a society in which censorship has often sought to regulate that speech. Such censorship has frequently occurred during times in which the nation has experienced the most rapid and dislocating changes. Thus, not only does censorship contradict the national tradition of free speech, but it also inhibits the process of understanding a changing society.

Contemporary America is such a changing society. It faces staggering change in nearly all aspects of its social life: an unpredictable economy in disarray, cities mired in violence and homelessness, embedded racial tensions erupting in neighborhood violence, and a political system that has lost the confidence of much of the public. Traditional values are also in a maelstrom, as exemplified by New York City's decision to distribute free condoms at its public schools. At the same time, many Americans are insecure about the cultural identity of the nation, in which the English language is being spoken by fewer immigrants and in which multiculturalists argue that traditional national holidays like Columbus Day and Thanksgiving are symbols of the country's oppressive past. In this era of insecurity, change, and confusion, censorship has proliferated. The music of black rap groups, the paintings of alternative lifestyle artists, and the Eurocentric history taught by white college professors have all come under attack by censorship advocates.

As multiculturalism replaces the older, more traditional social model of Americanized homogeneity, speech and censorship will increasingly form the ethnic and cultural battleground of this change. The controversies over bilingualism and Afrocentrism reflect this cultural battleground. Yet it is a national blessing that these cultural conflicts in the United States occur primarily in the realm of speech rather than, as has been the recent case in Eastern Europe, in violent battles in the streets. In America, speech has been that unique element that both defines a people's effort to live together in some kind of commonality, as well as the individual's attempt to retain some separate identity from the society at large. However, the ability of speech to perform these roles has lately been undermined by a rising tide of censorship.

During the last decade, censorship has become an increasingly prevalent force in American life. Its occurrences may not be as dramatic as some of the censorship controversies in the 1960s, when all of society seemed to be thrown into turmoil; nonetheless, censorship during the 1980s and 1990s has come from more diverse sources and has touched more kinds of speech than the censorship of the 1960s ever did. In fact, an award-winning documentary about recent censorship incidents in the United States has itself become embroiled in a censorship dispute and has been withheld from distribution.[1]

This book sets out to understand American censorship. By examining the various instances and examples of contemporary censorship, it explores the social forces motivating censorship campaigns. Although censorship has long occurred in American life, and although it has been defeated many times, it continues to surface with each generation. In a nation of free speech, censorship has been a constantly recurring social phenomenon. The following chapters attempt to explain the reasons for and social motivations behind the recurrent censorship impulse. And by understanding censorship, perhaps a fuller understanding can be acquired of American society, which has historically been defined and characterized by the speech of its citizens.

While innumerable works have dealt with the ongoing debate over whether certain speech should be censored and whether censorship is a valuable or destructive social tool, few have attempted to discover the fundamental causes underlying the censorship impulse in America. With the continual recurrence of censorship, many scholars and observers have documented the types of censorship that have occurred, the kinds of expressions censored, and the identity of the advocates of that censorship. Yet despite all the arguments over censorship and the evidentiary analysis of the incidents of censorship, there has been very little discussion of the uniquely American causes and motivations of its censorship activities. And though we often explore the national characteristic of free speech, we fail to examine the flip-side, the dark side of free speech – the preoccupation with censorship. Without such an understanding, however, we can never escape the generational repetition of censorship.

An essential condition for exploring censorship is to first define and understand the term as it will be used throughout this book. Under the constitutional definition of censorship, as employed in First Amendment cases, only government restriction of, or interference with, the content of speech qualifies as censorship. Such restrictions are in turn forbidden by the First Amendment. However, the Constitution clearly does not forbid an individual from prohibiting certain words or even any speech at all in her own home. Indeed, such informal rules exist in most family homes. Though this informal or unofficial censorship carries no legal penalties and is not recognized by the law as censorship, it often constitutes the social seed of government-sanctioned censorship. In a democracy, censorship laws or government-sanctioned censorship acts often arise from social movements or desires for such restrictions on speech. While these movements and desires, short of official government action, involve no violation of the First Amendment and do not legally qualify as censorship, they nonetheless often constitute a necessary prerequisite for government repression of speech. Thus, such unofficial censorship, as well as the more official brand of government censorship, shall be the focus of this book.

This broader definition of censorship is necessary to explore the social causes of the censorship impulse. In a democratic society, the eventual efforts of government to conduct some censorship activity – the kind forbidden by the First Amendment – result from the collective political pressure of many private individuals and groups calling for such action. Governmental restrictions on speech, like most other governmental actions, usually arise from popular pressures. Therefore, an understanding of censorship in America cannot be obtained simply by examining official acts of government censorship; it requires a look at how such censorship movements emerge and develop in society.

To explore the most basic causes of any censorship impulse in a democratic society, which initially emerges from certain social forces acting on the populace, censorship must be broadly defined as any organized social campaign to exclude or deny particular speech from public expression. Consequently, the broader definition of censorship used throughout the following chapters refers to any social crusade or activity that attempts to control the content of public discourse or to restrict the amount of speech entering the social stream of communication. Examples of such recent censorship crusades include the politically correct movement; the crusade against certain types of advertising; the campaigns against flag-burning and the National Endowment for the Arts; and public demands for restrictions on certain kinds of art, music, and television programming.

Censorship has been like a pesky disease throughout history. Due to the antidote of the First Amendment, it has not been fatal; and most outbreaks have been eventually cured. Yet the goal is to stop it from even arising and to relieve society from having to go through the convulsions before the cure. The drug of the First Amendment alone cannot accomplish this. Instead, we have to identify and understand the causes of censorship – not just address and cure the symptoms. For only an understanding of the social causes of censorship will illuminate the cure for future recurrence.

Throughout history, we have learned to fight censorship, but we have not learned to understand it. And because of this, censorship keeps coming back. The discussion in chapter 1 addresses the paradox of censorship in America – its continued existence in a nation dedicated to free speech and robust communication. It notes the generational recurrence of censorship, despite the historic pattern of futility. In particular, the censorship crusades of the 1990s are being waged by the generation that opposed all censorship in the 1960s.

As a prelude to analyzing the causes of contemporary censorship, the analysis in chapter 2 debunks the frequently asserted explanation that censorship results from a uniquely American intolerant antagonism to individual freedom. In refuting this explanation, this chapter examines the degree of freedom existing in American society and considers the historic advocates of censorship.

Chapter 3 addresses the social need to understand and resolve the causes of the censorship impulse. It argues that, in addition to the adverse effect on free speech, censorship distracts the nation from other more pressing social problems and consequently erodes public confidence in the political system.

Chapter 4 begins an analysis of the causes of censorship, arguing that a changing concept and treatment of truth has in turn made the nation more tolerant of censorship. By examining how truth is treated in the judicial, political, and educational arenas, truth seems to have become more political and ideological and less a rational product of free speech and inquiry. As exemplified by the politically correct movement, censorship becomes more tolerable since the attainment of truth is not perceived to depend on the free expression of ideas.

Chapter 5 analyzes censorship as an attempt to define American identity. In a nation of immigrants and with no inherited social identity, speech has often been the primary means for forming and expressing national identity. Consequently, censorship becomes more an attempt to influence social identity than a restriction against individual liberty. Such recent censorship campaigns as the flag-desecration statutes illustrate the battle over speech as the battle over national identity.

Recently, many censorship attempts rest on the claim that certain speech amounts to action and that if not controlled, that speech will inevitably lead to harmful social acts. Examples include campaigns to censor certain advertising, various kinds of racist and sexist speech, and a wide array of speech to which children are exposed. Chapter 6 addresses this type of censorship activity and analyzes the reasons why speech is coming to be treated as action in our contemporary media society. Similarly, chapter 7 notes how certain contemporary censorship attempts erupt from a desire to limit or control the vast amount of speech now existing in the information age. It examines censorship as a social desire to impose certain quality standards on its public speech.

A common libertarian explanation for the occurrence of censorship is that it comes from communities that become too strong and consequently too intolerant of individual freedoms. The discussion in chapter 8, however, contradicts this assertion. It argues that censorship more frequently occurs in weak and unstable communities. Likewise, chapter 9 asserts that censorship often expresses certain social insecurities and fears. Rather than an act of overzealous national confidence and arrogance, censorship attempts frequently resemble a desperate attempt to calm social insecurities and anxieties.

Throughout American history, censorship has usually been viewed as a remedy for distasteful or disturbing speech. Unfortunately, it has rarely been seen for what it most fundamentally is: a destroyer of the cherished American freedom and exercise of speech. Yet eventually most censorship attempts have been remembered as regrettable mistakes.

In a diverse and changing society, speech is often the only true reflection of society and the only recorder of the memories and history of that society. According to the melting pot metaphor, only the unrestrained mix of all the voices in society can record an accurate history of America. Therefore, and particularly as America becomes increasingly multicultural, censorship threatens the fullness of the American memory. Unless we understand it and resolve it, censorship will continually dampen the vitality of American life.

1

The Mystery of Contradictions

With the passage of time, the acquisition of a little knowledge through experience, and a second chance, society can sometimes avoid repeating the same mistakes. This is the optimism of history. Indeed, some mistakes, like Prohibition, America has made only once. Others have been corrected on a second effort. After World War II, for instance, the United States and its allies knew from their experience of World War I that they could not let the defeated nations of Germany and Japan slide into political and economic chaos. History had taught that only prosperity and stability brought lasting peace.

Still other lessons have required more time and more failures to learn. One such lesson has been that of equality. Over the last two centuries, America has painfully learned that its first impulse was right – that all persons are created equal. We are also learning that our environment and our children need special protection. And we have learned, perhaps finally, that even banks can go broke.

Though the optimistic side of history promises progress, its pessimistic side warns of protracted stalemates and repetitious errors. Unfortunately, some problems seem condemned to be repeated by each generation. The recurrence of greed and aggression may never disappear. Yet this repetition is at least somewhat understandable – someone always benefits rather directly and immediately from the exercise of greed. Censorship, however, seems a far less understandable repetition, if only because the benefits or pleasures of censorship often appear so vague.

As it prepares to enter the twenty-first century, the United States has not yet escaped the recurring cycle of censorship. It has not yet learned the lesson that censorship is fruitless and often destructive. This failure occurs despite the lessons learned by, and the proclamations of, the judiciary. Since adoption of the Bill of Rights two hundred years ago, our judicial institutions have come to understand the lesson that much of the rest of the world is struggling with now: Individual freedom must constitute the foundation of any healthy and progressive society. This lesson, of course, did not come easily or quickly.

It took the Supreme Court nearly a half century to conclude that political speech, no matter how critical of the government, could not be censored. In 1919, Justice Oliver Wendell Holmes, in his famous dissent in *Abrams v. United States* argued that individuals should be free to criticize their government even during times of war. Though the Court did not follow Holmes's advice, it did in 1931 rule that the government could not stop publication – or exercise prior restraint – of information with which it disagreed or opposed. In the 1960s, the Supreme Court finally realized Holmes's wisdom and held that individuals could not be prosecuted under antisedition or antisubversive statutes for their criticism of the government or their advocacy of unpopular ideas such as socialism and communism. These types of statutes had been passed in 1798, in 1918, and again in 1950, and the Court finally ruled that their censorship effect was unconstitutional. The optimism of history had prevailed.

Although the courts have learned lessons from the experience of past censorship activities, much of the American public apparently has not. The contemporary assaults on free speech are "coming not so much from the Supreme Court as from local officials, corporations, government agencies and citizen groups."[1] Just as Americans banned the books of James Joyce and D. H. Lawrence in the 1920s and called for censorship of movies in the 1930s and of television and rock music in the 1960s and 1970s, so too are many Americans in the 1990s seeking censorship of disturbing or disagreeable speech.

During just the last several years, censorship crusades have occurred on nearly every level and aspect of American life. Congress has grappled with censorship matters in the National Endowment for the Arts (NEA) and flag-burning controversies. Universities have enacted speech codes and have censored politically incorrect ideas. Cities have tried to ban speech that is offensive to various groups of people, including prohibitions on swearing. Local prosecutors have tried to censor disclosure of information about public court cases, such as the identity of victims of certain crimes. Artists and their creations have been censored. The Robert Mapplethorpe exhibit, the photographs of which were the subject of a highly publicized obscenity trial in Cincinnati, was the most notorious; but in another case a San Francisco photographer who took pictures of men and women nude with their children underwent a nine-week grand jury investigation. Music groups like 2 Live Crew have been subject to obscenity prosecutions; others have had to place warning stickers on their album jackets. Television, as always, came under fire for its purportedly indecent programming. And a New Jersey judge even banned a movie company from filming scenes of *The Bonfire of the Vanities* in a county courthouse because he objected to one scene in which a riot occurred after a judicial ruling.

Censorship campaigns in recent years, in addition to reaching new kinds of speech, have also continued in some traditional directions. Book censorship has been one such focus. A 1988 report by the Office for Intellectual Freedom of the American Library Association stated that challenges to library books and school materials increased by 168 percent in the previous five years. And People for the American Way found that attempts to censor school books doubled in the Northeast between 1988 and 1989.

The book censorship that began in the 1920s continues to flourish in the 1990s. Among the books that came under attack in 1989 were *The Hobbit, Of Mice and Men, The Catcher in the Rye, The Color Purple, Catch-22, Slaughterhouse-Five* and even *Little Red Riding Hood.* Two books frequently censored, *To Kill a Mockingbird* and *The Lord of the Rings,* were recently listed among America's ten most influential books.[2] According to Arthur Kropp, president of People for the American Way, "The censorship movement is flourishing in America."[3] Consequently, censorship was targeted as a pressing issue by the nation's booksellers at the American Booksellers Association's ninetieth annual convention. On April 23, 1990, the association placed a full-page advertisement in thirty newspapers to protest increasing censorship efforts.

In addition to book censorship, attempts at television censorship have continued. Despite the popularity of such controversial television shows as "L.A. Law" and "Saturday Night Live," legislation imposing a complete ban on "indecent programming," which could well have applied to those shows, was recently introduced in Congress.

This flurry of censorship activity not only ignores America's commitment to free speech and the courts' prohibition of censorship, it has also come from people who should know better. Indeed, the current censorship advocacy comes frequently from persons who earlier in their lives stood on the opposite side of the censorship question.

The generation of the 1960s, for instance, must have continually resolved to themselves, as their parents and teachers tried so haplessly

to censor the music and books of the time, that they would never attempt such blatant censorship of the books and music of their children's generation. Yet the generation that saw the censorship of
popular but irreverent television programs like "Laugh-In" and "The
Smothers Brothers Comedy Hour" now seeks to impose "decency" standards on television programming.

Throughout the 1960s, popular music was constantly battling censorship. At Ed Sullivan's insistence, The Rolling Stones changed the
lyric "Let's spend the night together" to "Let's spend some time together." The Jefferson Airplane was repeatedly fined for failing to com-
ply with performance contract clauses that prohibited "verbal abuse."
And Country Joe McDonald was fined for using profane language during a performance. Instances of such censorship are now often re-
counted with pride and enthusiasm by the people who grew up during
that era—they have become a generation's folk tales. Oliver Stone's
movie *The Doors* reflects that generational pride in its scene depicting
the 1969 concert where Jim Morrison was arrested for obscenity.

Yet despite this earlier experience with censorship, there exists today across the nation a widespread campaign to censor certain types of
popular music. According to one music critic, "[Pop music's] most important public appearances took place in courtrooms rather than concert halls, [as] prosecutors and legislators fulminated over the dangers
of pop lyrics about sex or suicide."[4] In one case, the leader of a well-
known West Coast political punk band called The Dead Kennedys was
arrested in 1987 under a statute forbidding the dissemination of harmful matter to minors for distributing a poster from the group's album.
More recently, Washington Governor Booth Gardner signed legislation
imposing criminal penalties on music store owners who sell recordings
with sexually explicit lyrics to minors,[5] and prosecutors in Omaha, Nebraska, filed obscenity charges against five record stores for selling the
2 Live Crew album, "Sports Weekend."[6] On a national scale, a prominent movement begun in the 1980s by Tipper Gore and Susan Baker,
which is more organized than any censorship campaign in the 1960s,
seeks to restrict music lyrics and regulate the distribution of certain
popular music. Indeed, the lobbying of Congress by Gore and Baker's
Parents Music Resource Center (PMRC) and the subsequent hearings
by the Senate Commerce Committee on popular music lyrics is the
closest that popular music has come to explicit government regulation.
Due to the efforts of PMRC and other groups, several states by 1990
had enacted laws requiring warning stickers on albums deemed to be
offensive.

These efforts at censorship are nothing new. Elvis Presley was
thought to be obscene in the 1950s. The effect of the censorship efforts

are also not new. As in generations past, censorship in the 1990s seems only to sensationalize the speech and give it even more notoriety.[7] This is almost an inevitable consequence of a media society. The arrest of 2 Live Crew on obscenity charges, for instance, served as an extremely effective promotional and sales tool for the group's album.[8] Indeed, the album sales of censored groups have practically kept the record industry afloat.[9] Similarly, the religious opposition to the movie *The Last Temptation of Christ* only seemed to increase attendance. The Mapplethorpe exhibit in Cincinnati attracted the largest attendance of any exhibit ever shown by the Cincinnati Contemporary Arts Center. And despite highly visible efforts to censor sexually oriented materials, a recent survey revealed that Americans are watching X-rated videos in record numbers.[10] Yet this boomerang effect has not appeared to inhibit the contemporary advocates of censorship.

The futility of censorship in a free society, however, is not a recent phenomenon. The heroic figures of eighteen-century Enlightenment ideas – Franklin, Jefferson, and Madison – realized from history that censorship reflected a superstitious and ignorant past, and inhibited social and scientific progress. Yet despite their efforts to eliminate official censorship by the church and state, and despite the promise of eighteenth-century Enlightenment ideas embodied in its Constitution, the United States has not abolished censorship. Though official state and church censors no longer exist, the impulse of censorship still beats strong in society. Censorship continues to exist despite its contradiction of the ideas underlying the birth of the United States and despite the repeated failures of censorship attempts throughout history.

The Federalist party of John Adams in 1798 imposed a law forbidding criticism of the government. Intended to silence the opposing voice of Jefferson's Democratic-Republican party, the law was the first national attempt at political censorship. The result, however, was exactly opposite the intention. Both Jefferson's followers and the American public were outraged at the law, and with the defeat of John Adams, the Federalist party never again achieved national power. Several decades later, in the 1830s and 1840s, proslavery forces in both the North and South tried to silence the abolitionist presses. Instead of making the slavery problem disappear, however, the resolution of the issue was simply delayed until a great civil war engulfed the country.

Twice in the twentieth century, in the wake of the two world wars, the nation enacted laws punishing those who advocated socialist or pacifist ideas. This censorship resulted from the fear that America would fall under Communist control. Not only was such a measure unnecessary, since the advocates of communism and socialism in America never numbered more than a small minority, but the collapse of the

Communist world in the late 1980s and of the Soviet Union itself in 1991 demonstrated that knowledge and popular opinion, not censorship, were the weapons to defeat totalitarianism.

The McCarthyism of the 1950s reflected one of the most bitter censorship crusades the country has ever known. It touched all areas of society, but it eventually proved to be nothing more than national paranoia. Its leader, Senator Joseph McCarthy, was himself eventually censured in the United States Senate. Yet in its course, McCarthyism inflicted great pain and trauma on a nation and particularly on the citizens it unfairly persecuted.

Perhaps the most futile censorship attempts occurred in the 1960s and 1970s. During that period, a new generation of American youth rebelled against a social censorship of untraditional values, alternative lifestyles, and radical ideas. However, the continued attempts to censor or control the rock and roll lyrics and artistic expressions of that generation only produced more antagonism to traditional values. Indeed, the clumsy and ultimately futile attempts at censorship in the 1960s are now ironically memorialized in the record collections of most forty year olds.

The censorship of movies in the 1970s illustrated another futile attempt to regulate speech. Memorable movies such as *The Last Picture Show* in 1973, *Carnal Knowledge* in 1972, and *Where Eagles Dare* in 1970 continued a long line of attempted censorships of movies, including *Birth of a Nation* in 1915, *Tomorrow's Children* in 1937, *The Outlaw* in 1946, *The Miracle* in 1951, *Baby Doll* in 1956, and *The Connection* in 1962.[11]

Despite these historical lessons, censorship erupted again during the decade of the 1980s and continues now into the 1990s. Increasingly, the courts are having to settle many of the censorship disputes. While very few cases relating to the banning of educational materials existed a decade ago, such cases are abundant today. Obscenity prosecutions doubled from 1987 to 1988, and then quadrupled from 1988 to 1989. At the same time, the federal courts overturned three highly visible national attempts at censorship: the attempt by Congress to control the kind of art funded by the NEA, the flag-desecration enactment by Congress, and the attempt by the Federal Communications Commission (FCC) to impose new decency standards on television and radio programming.

Although the courts consistently rule against government censorship, they are not stopping the censorship drive in society. In fact, the increased censorship litigation reflects an underlying increase in censorship activity in society.

This increase in censorship activity reflects some unique aspects of the current trend of censorship. Contemporary censorship tends to flow up from the grassroots of society rather than down from a social elite or the traditional leaders of censorship in society. Neither the government nor the long-established religious groups are leading the way. Instead, the proliferation of censorship in the last several years has been accompanied by confusion and double-talk in the nation's leadership. Although President George Bush praised free speech as "the most fundamental and deeply revered of all our liberties" in a speech condemning the political correctness movement on college campuses, he had entered the White House with a campaign against free speech that featured his advocacy of a flag-burning amendment and his derision of "card-carrying members of the ACLU." And later in his administration he acquiesced in the crusade against the NEA.[12]

As cultural issues relating to speech and art increasingly become political issues, more and more people will be drawn into the censorship struggle. As the diversity of individuals joining censorship campaigns has increased, censorship is no longer only the practice of moral conservative groups. On the contrary, liberal or leftist groups such as feminist and civil rights organizations have joined the campaign. In seeking to end sexism and violence against women, many feminists advocate censorship of the speech they claim promotes such activity, and in seeking to combat racism and prejudice, civil rights groups have tried to wipe out the type of speech they claim fosters an inferior image of minority groups. Even the liberally oriented academic community has resorted to censorship of speech deemed to be politically incorrect. This liberal addition to contemporary censorship campaigns marks a sharp distinction from those of the past.

As reflected by these quasi-liberal censorship campaigns, the cultural tensions in contemporary society contribute to censorship activity. Moreover, the current preoccupation with censorship ironically coincides with a uniquely American fascination with speech.

Common stereotypes hold that the Japanese are compulsive workers and the French take pride in their culinary culture. America's notoriety, however, lies in its speech—it is a society of speakers. Throughout history, speech has defined and shaped social life in the United States. From soapboxes and penny press newspapers in the nineteenth century to television talk shows and camcorders in the present era, the prevalent activity of Americans has been expressing themselves. It is one mark of American culture that has remained constant.

The country was described as a rural paradise in the eighteenth century, as the land of railroads and vast western ranches in the nineteenth century, and as the nation of the steel mill and automobile factory in the early twentieth century. But none of these descriptions holds true today. Indeed, the only description that fits each historical period is that of abundant speech—America is and always has been the land of

overflowing speech. More newspapers, magazines, books, and television programs are produced and consumed here than anywhere else in
the world. Those especially talented at expression receive the most national attention and of course the greatest financial reward. The actors
and actresses, the musicians, the television news anchors and talk
show hosts live in the mansions of their speech.

The United States may no longer produce the most desired automo-
biles nor the most brilliant color television sets. But it still unquestionably produces the most speech. Throughout the day, the telephone lines
carry hundreds of millions of conversations and the television and radio talk shows play to audiences of millions. Long after the shops and
factories close for the day, and long after the restaurants and theaters
close for the night, the cities still ring with speech. A late night walk
down a nearly deserted city street is interrupted by trucks dropping off
bundles of newspapers and magazines for the next day's readers. The
darkness of the night is broken by the lights of the billboards. Though
the door to one's home can be closed to the city outside, with the push
of a button the quiet home can quickly be linked to the world of
speech—the television never goes silent. It gives us everything from C-
SPAN to MTV.

Speech marks the stages of life. The first joyous witness of a new life
comes with the first screams of a newborn baby. The first spoken
words, the first recital in school, the vow of marriage, the job interview,
the first parent-child conversation about sex, and the stories of remem-
brance told to grandchildren all mark the passage through life.

Speech also characterizes our public rituals. We celebrate national
holidays with public speeches. Our democratic process revolves around
the campaign speech. And before our leaders assume their duties and
powers, they must take an oath of office. Indeed, one of the requirements and tests of our social and public leaders is that they lead with
their speech. Rarely will a politician be respected or supported if she
cannot make an inspiring speech.

Not only does speech define the American character, it financially
supports us. Though we do not export much steel, we do export compact discs of American music groups and videotapes of American movies. Though we no longer sell television sets abroad, we do distribute
television programming worldwide. Though our paper and forest product exports have greatly decreased, we still produce and deliver to the
world the most books and magazines. A visit abroad brings many new
and different sights, but one very familiar and consistent sight is that
of movie theaters playing American movies. Despite its trade deficit,
the one shining American export is speech and entertainment. In this
area, the United States clearly dominates the world market. Every year
foreign consumers spend $300 million on movie tickets, compact discs,
videotapes, and other American entertainment products.

Perhaps because of this economic might of speech, Americans also ascribe great remedial power to speech. For the most complex and deeply rooted social problems, speech often becomes the perceived remedy. If we prohibit panhandling and the sale of sexually explicit material on our streets, the problems of the homeless and of sexual violence will somehow go away. Cities will be cleaned up and renovated if just the graffiti is washed away. The drug problems can be cured if everyone "just says no."

This perceived power of speech is reflected in our most important national document, the Constitution. It not only guarantees the right to speak, but confers the right to remain silent when accused of a crime: the sword of a person's speech cannot be used against him. The power of speech has also been depicted in the American cultural symbols and national myths. The triumph of Jimmy Stewart's passionate filibuster in *Mr. Smith Goes to Washington,* for instance, reflects an American belief in the strength and purity of speech.

Yet for all the value and importance we place on speech, we are also quick in our vindictiveness against it. Speech can be the subject of punishment almost as much as it can be the object of admiration. Indeed, the punishment of speech has become an American trait almost as much as has the elevation and prominence of speech. For instance, although a politician's job is essentially one of debate, we punish errant officials with silence. We do not impose money fines or force them to stand for early election when they violate certain rules or codes of behavior; instead, we censure them — we take away the role they were chosen to perform. Such censure, from Senator Joseph McCarthy in 1956 to Senator David Durenburger in 1990, has become the most common punishment for senatorial violations of ethical rules. Censure has become a common form of punishment in all areas of American life. When Andy Rooney allegedly said something offensive about gays, he was taken off the air — censured — for an appropriate punishment time.

Although we demand a robust consumer economy that produces all products we could possibly want, we react against its rampant materialism and against the products we don't like by censoring the economic speech of advertising. And though we display our recognition of maturity in children by letting them join the conversation of adults, we show our displeasure by censure. While children are now taught to express their feelings, they are punished with time-outs that impose solitude and silence.

For all that we value speech, we are thus quick to silence it. Speech, like romantic love, inspires immediate action. Perhaps it is what is closest to our human sensibilities. We wash off the graffiti before we even contemplate the message. We remove the bumper sticker from a newly purchased used car before we check the oil. The inadvertent profanity of a talk show host incites more intense reaction than does a shooting or robbery down the block. We insist that students raise their hands before speaking in class, even when half the students do not bother to show up.

Speech occupies a central role in our daily lives. It is the staple of a human interaction, as attested to by the booming industry of hearing aids. It is the focus of our fantasies, as reflected in the possibility that speech might exist in the most unexpected of creatures, just as it did with a horse in the television show "Mr. Ed," with a baby in the movie *Look Who's Talking*, and even with inanimate objects as in Tom Robbins's novel *Skinny Legs and All*. It is also our depiction of reality, and perhaps by changing the image we think we can change everything else. And so we censor. But the muzzle of censorship never really silences the speech.

The recurrence of censorship in America has followed a somewhat generational pattern. Speech becomes each generation's mark or identity, and censorship becomes the attempt of the older to build a bridge of agreement or continuity with the younger generation. This generational cycle continually repeats: The young generation breaks away and creates its own sense of identity through the speech of its generation – the books, the music, and the art. Meanwhile, the older generation seeks to retain its authority and control through censorship.

The identity of generations has come from their unique forms of speech. In the 1920s, the writers of the Lost Generation and the musicians of the Jazz Age defined the new generation. The generation of the 1950s had Elvis Presley and a new kind of music called rock and roll. In the 1960s, the hippies and the protestors, the rock bands and the rebellious writers all helped to define a new generation. Indeed, throughout modern history the lyrics of popular music have played an empowering and generational role for youth.[13] The rock music of the 1960s and 1970s, like today's rap music, rebelled against the authority of the establishment and attempted to create a generational identity for its listeners. The music pushed to the limits that which had been designated as taboo by the older generation, and it endured as the generation's music as long as it continued to flaunt social rules and authority.

In the 1990s, rap music and heavy metal rock and roll are the younger generation's music. Both break away from the older generation, and both have consequently been under heavy censorship pressure. Contemporary heavy metal rock and its raw lyrics have become the nightmare of most parents. Metal musicians have acquired a cultlike audience and play on the themes of wild rebellion and disillusionment with the older, corrupt generation. The lyrics are blatantly antiestablishment and voice the anger and dissatisfaction of mostly middle-class youths. Likewise, the lyrics of rap music also attract youths seeking to break with the rules and norms of the older generation.

The decline of censorship activity, like the narrowing of the generation gap, cannot occur without an understanding of the reasons for its occurrence. The generation gap is often narrowed through communication, not punishment. Similarly, the key to resolving the puzzling persistence of censorship lies in a greater understanding achieved through more speech, not through the further silencing of some voices.

The nature and characteristics of contemporary censorship, as with each generation of censorship, are both unique and somewhat historically patterned. The traditional explanation offered by its opponents for the occurrence of censorship does not fit contemporary patterns. The usual libertarian explanation for American censorship points to a consistent strain of reactionary intolerance and antifreedom impulses in the national character. According to this argument, censorship stems from the intolerably repressive nature of American society. This simplistic answer, however, does not explain the current censorship activities of certain liberal groups including feminist and civil rights organizations.

The libertarian analysis regarding the causes of American censorship took shape in eras when America was primarily concerned with national security issues and when the government assumed the role of primary censor. Many past censorship campaigns focused on political speech and occurred during times of national security crises, particularly during and immediately following the two world wars. At the present time, however, the United States is in no apparent military danger and faces no pressing threat to national security. Most of the current censorship attempts involve not political speech, but cultural and artistic speech such as music, art, and the flag. Furthermore, many of the attempts are not being led primarily by traditional agents such as the government or established religious organizations. Despite the increased politicization of artistic speech, the government has lately tried to avoid any direct censorship role with regard to music, art, and motion pictures. Even such a traditional censor as the Catholic church has lessened its role in enforcing moral standards with respect to the kinds of movies viewed by its members.

Given the American love of and fascination with speech, the underlying cause of all censorship attempts does not appear to be an antispeech attitude prevalent in society. Instead, censorship attempts may result from a fear of the destructive power of certain speech and reflect a desperate move to release society from being a hostage to such speech. Furthermore, since America's identity is defined by the speech of the time, perhaps censorship reflects a fear that if society indulges, for instance, violent and degrading speech, the society itself will become more coarse, brutal, and indifferent. If speech, one of the most human of activities, is allowed to become debasing and dehumanizing, then perhaps life will follow.

Censorship issues often touch the emotional nerve of society. Controversies like flag-burning and sexually explicit art fire the most intense of social passions. Unquestionably, censorship involves speech with which we are most uncomfortable. Yet after the emotions cool, we realize that censorship destroys the most cherished and distinctive of American characteristics — speech.

Looking back into our national memory, we see that censorship has existed throughout one of the greatest social experiments with freedom. It has occurred in the midst of freedom; it has not occupied or filled an absence of freedom. Censorship has instead arisen in a society of unprecedented freedom struggling to define itself and its future. Thus, its causes lie deep in the social fabric, and not simply within a strain of intolerance existing in the national mindset.

Censorship in a Nation of Freedom

Censorship cannot be explained by describing the United States as a nation hostile to freedom and intolerant of diverse debate, particularly since the country has become home to the greatest diversity of immigrants and ethnic groups the world has ever witnessed. Instead, the occurrence of censorship attempts actually reflects the remarkable degree of freedom present in society. For instance, the unsuccessful attempts to stop a Nazi demonstration several years ago in a Jewish neighborhood in Skokie, Illinois, only revealed the substantial degree of freedom available even to those who espouse the most unpopular of ideas. Indeed, censorship attempts achieve notoriety primarily because they contrast with the prevailing attitudes of freedom.

Political scientists and legal scholars may debate the degree of freedom present in American society, but most people have fairly strong opinions on the freedom they believe they possess. Some of the most common expressions made in casual conversation or in heated argument include: "It's a free country"; "Well, you're entitled to your own opinion"; and, of course, "You can't tell me what to do."

Whether they are or not, most citizens feel that they are free. The public appeal of the gun lobby and its banner of the freedom to own a gun, as well as the harsh reactions of people to any restrictions on their freedom to drive and travel, demonstrate the emotional hold of freedom on the American soul. In the United States, as the movies preach, anything can happen and anyone can say whatever he wants. Indeed, according to many social critics, the current problems in society do not arise from restrictions on individual freedom, but stem from various excesses of certain types of freedoms.

As the oldest democracy on earth, political freedom has flourished here longer than in any other country. In addition to democratic political freedoms, Americans also enjoy the wide exercise of individual freedoms. Among those are the freedoms of religion, association, privacy, speech, and press. These liberties help construct a tolerant society of relatively free and diverse individuals.

Since Roger Williams departed from Massachusetts Bay Colony to start his own settlement in what is now Rhode Island, religious tolerance has been both a legal and cultural principle. Although the early Puritans envisioned a society unified in the Puritan beliefs, it soon became a place of extraordinary religious diversity. From all across Europe came denominations of many kinds. Consequently, one of the constitutional aims of the movement for independence was the prevention of any established church in America, particularly the Anglican Church of England.

In addition to the proliferation of sects in America, the religious activity of Americans has always been intense. The Enlightenment movements in both the eighteenth and nineteenth centuries, just as the evangelical movements today, revealed the vast public enthusiasm for religion and religious activity. This activity has also translated into political activity, as various religions have taken part in political reform movements such as abolitionism and antimonopolism of the nineteenth century and the child welfare, social justice, and civil rights movements of the twentieth century.

The courts have long upheld the free exercise of religious beliefs, even though that exercise may conflict with certain secular values and practices. For instance, a child cannot be expelled from school for refusing to salute the flag if such an act would violate the child's religious beliefs. Nor can a person be forced to recite an oath that includes the phrase "so help me God" if that oath infringes on the person's spiritual beliefs. The Supreme Court has ruled that if an individual is discharged from her job because her religious beliefs do not allow her to work on Saturday, that individual cannot be denied unemployment compensation benefits. Furthermore, compulsory school attendance laws cannot be enforced against children for whom such attendance would violate their religious beliefs. Even statutes forbidding fortune-telling have been held to not apply against persons whose religious exercise would be infringed. And, of course, persons who object to war on religious grounds cannot be forced to perform military duties or service. Even mandatory ROTC for public high school students has been held unconstitutional as applied to conscientious objectors.

While the courts have forged great protections for the sanctity of religious beliefs, the exercise of religious freedom in America is demonstrated by the number of Americans actively involved in religious activity and the coexistence of widely diverse sects and beliefs. As of 1990, for example, church membership in the United States totaled more than 145 million, and this is not counting those who practice their religious beliefs but who are not official members of any church.[1] As of 1987, there were approximately 349,381 different types of churches in this country.[2]

Ecumenism, or the blending of religions, has become an integral facet of a pluralistic society. Americans walk the same streets to different churches and eat in the same restaurants after their different religious services. They are not divided by religious denominations, but are generally unified in their respect for religious beliefs. On September 22, 1991, for instance, the Reverend Billy Graham spoke to a crowd of 250,000 in New York's Central Park—a crowd comprising Jews, Baptists, and persons from nearly every other denomination. Cardinal John O'Connor had even urged New York Catholics to attend.

In addition to religious freedom, Americans also enjoy the seemingly polar privileges of privacy and association. Possessing not just the personal ability to say no to any outside involvement, persons also possess a constitutional right of privacy from certain governmental intrusions. Furthermore, countless statutes give privacy rights in a wide array of circumstances, such as data privacy acts. Hence, Americans are as free to be left alone as they are to join with others in a wide range of voluntary associations. And join they have done.

Alexis de Tocqueville first observed in the nineteenth century the American impulse to gather together in voluntary associations, and this propensity has continued to the present. Currently, more than twenty-two thousand nonreligious, noncommercial organizations exist in the United States.[3] Seven out of ten Americans belong to at least one association, and one out of four belong to four or more associations. As with the great diversity of religious sects, the complex web of social organizations helps create in America a society of great pluralism and tolerance toward diversity.

Of all the constitutional freedoms, perhaps the most prominent and exercised are the freedoms of speech and press. These are perhaps the most American of all this nation's freedoms. As Winston Churchill observed in 1945, "nowhere [in the world] is speech freer" than in the United States. This freedom has indeed long characterized American society.

The colonists' exercise of speech and press freedoms paved the way for the break with England and facilitated the formation of a new constitutional democracy. Once society experienced the exhilaration of freedom of expression, it used it more than it had ever been used before.

Even before breaking with England, America had more printing presses and newspapers than any country in the world. And after the Revolutionary War and the achievement of national independence, newspapers exploded in popularity. For instance, during the period from 1783 to 1801, 450 newspapers were started.

Throughout the last two centuries, and particularly in the last several decades, the media and communications industries in the United States have greatly expanded. From 1947 to 1970, for instance, the amount of newsprint consumption more than doubled; and from 1950 to 1970 the number of published books more than tripled, after having increased fivefold since 1880.[4] During the two-decade span from 1950 to 1970, the number of radio stations more than doubled, and the number of television stations increased by a multiple of eight.[5] The number of cable television stations more than doubled during the decade of the 1980s, after a sevenfold increase since 1960.[6] The number of subscribers to cable and pay television also tripled during the 1980s.[7] And during the single year of 1988, there occurred on average approximately 1.7 billion telephone conversations every day.[8]

The explosion of these forms of communication has reflected the importance of speech in American history and society. Nearly all of the dramatic and momentous events of American history have flowed from the igniting spirit of free expression. The movement for national independence was inspired by the profound language of the Declaration of Independence. From the abolitionists came the spark for the Civil War; from the rallying cries of the union organizers came the beginnings of the working class movement; and from the rhetoric of reformers came the impulse for the progressive and New Deal reforms. The demonstrations of the civil rights movement, the women's movement, and the nuclear freeze movement all fed off of the power of public speech.

Even as the power of expression provided the fuel for American social progress, the courts solidified the protections for those who wished to advocate even the most unpopular of ideas. Radical socialist and Communist advocacy was protected, as was the publication of vulgar and disgusting words. As a result, the United States has become a country in which anyone can say just about anything. Indeed, a common complaint about the modern press is that it has become too free and that it enjoys immense power without any corresponding duties or accountability.

Because of the virtual sanctity of free speech, anyone can criticize the government, the courts, or the corporations. And they frequently do. Government and business leaders certainly have no immunity from criticism. It often seems almost unfashionable for journalists and scholars to speak with too much praise of any public figure. Vietnam and Watergate firmly established the practice of government criticism, and with the recent exposés of the personal lives of public figures, the adversarial relationship between press and government continues.[9] Investigative journalism, with an eye toward exposing corruption and abuse in government, remains highly popular and is frequently employed. As a result, a host of new investigative reporting programs, all modeled somewhat loosely after "60 Minutes," have appeared on television.

One barometer of speech freedoms in society is whether those freedoms exist even in times of national crisis. War is one such crisis. Every recent military engagement has been met with intense and vocal criticism, along with, of course, government efforts to censor that criticism.

The freedom of speech during wartime has significantly expanded since the prosecutions under the World War I Espionage and Sedition Acts occurred. During the Vietnam conflict, the *New York Times* published the Pentagon Papers despite intense opposition from the government. The lawsuit brought and eventually dropped by General William Westmoreland against CBS also demonstrated the type of press freedom enjoyed during the conflict. President Carter's attempted rescue of the Iran hostages was heavily criticized, as were President Reagan's military excursions into Central America and the Middle East. Throughout the 1980s the nuclear freeze movement continually held rallies at military bases and tried to upset the transportation of nuclear weapons. And President Bush's decision to wage war against Iraq attracted much opposition by both the public and the United States Senate, which hotly debated Bush's decision to commit military troops. After the military confrontation ended, criticism reappeared regarding Bush's peace agreements.

Throughout this century, freedoms of speech and press have followed an expansive evolution. Though organized protests have occurred during nearly every period of history, they are a regular event now. During the first ten months of 1991, for instance, the New York Department of Parks and Recreation had issued 260 permits for protests at the United Nations site alone. Groups of people now demonstrate in protest against everything from Catholic church rules on the priesthood to government tax increases to Columbus Day celebrations. Controversial figures like the Reverend Al Sharpton attract demonstrations wherever they go. Community tensions are sometimes pushed to the breaking point with public demonstrations on such highly emotional issues as abortion and gay rights. Yet even a protestor burning the flag at the Republican party's convention is now free from punishment or state interference.

In addition to these traditional ways of public expression, new opportunities for speech are emerging and promise to facilitate the flow of more and more speech through society. While the book and newspaper publishing businesses offered the only means of mass communication a century ago, a host of electronic and telecommunications technologies now allow Americans to communicate with each other in many different forms. Fax machines, cable television, computer communication networks, electronic mail, and telecommunications services such as the 900 network and conferencing capabilities all provide for speech in ways that were unavailable a decade ago.

This brief examination of America's freedoms and the exercise of its speech rights demonstrates the high level of tolerance and libertarianism present in the social fabric. Indeed, this fabric of freedom allows the most ethnically and culturally diverse society in the world to maintain social peace. Though at times Americans doubt the tolerance and freedom of their society, they need only look at the rest of the world to at least relatively settle their doubts. For instance, as Europe's ethnic mix changes with immigration, those countries have discovered that they are not as tolerant as they once thought they were. The world has also witnessed the rise of ethnic hate speech in France and Germany and the increase in cultural warfare in former Yugoslavia. The Gulf War demonstrated the intolerance and rigidity of the Arab states. The Tiananmen Square massacre once again revealed the tyranny of Communist rule. As rigid Communist rule ends in Eastern Europe and the former Soviet Union, those regions are experiencing intense ethnic conflicts within their own borders. Even Canada is struggling to reconcile the separatist demands of French-speaking Quebec. Yet as the rest of the world is drifting toward separation and division of people by ethnic or religious groupings, the United States is continuing its great experiment with integration and pluralism.

Even so enlightened a country as Great Britain engages in restraints that appear massive to one accustomed to life under the First Amendment. The press there is hobbled by threats of contempt for publishing virtually anything about criminal trials. An international human rights organization reported recently that the British government had dramatically eroded press freedoms and increased its powers of censorship.[10]

On the basis of this comparison with other countries, the United States would most surely be described as a free and tolerant society. And so the recurrence of censorship cannot simply be attributed to a repressive society or government. Of course, this is not to claim that the United States is a perfectly open, free, and tolerant society – rather, it is only to say that, when measured against the rest of the world, it certainly cannot be labeled as an unfree society.

This national freedom, however, has developed out of a history of conflict. And this history of conflict also tells the story of censorship in

America – for the history of censorship mirrors the history of freedom. Thus, the existence of censorship crusades often indicates the presence and exercise of freedom, because without freedom there would be no demand for the restriction of it through censorship.

Since the birth of the nation, the crusades for censorship and freedom have existed alongside each other. Moreover, those advocating censorship have also been the freedom-fighters on different issues and at different times. For instance, the Puritans who created the first American model of democracy with the Mayflower Compact later became intolerant repressors during the witchcraft trials at Salem. Subsequently, the patriots of Boston seeking freedom from British rule did not hesitate to burn the presses of Tory sympathizers with whom they disagreed. Even after the war for independence and the widespread distribution of its manifesto of freedom, the Declaration of Independence, the Federalist party under President John Adams obtained passage of the Alien and Sedition Acts of 1798, which attempted to silence any criticism levied against it by Thomas Jefferson's emerging Republican-Democratic party. Of course, Jefferson, the author of the eloquent statement of freedom in the Declaration of Independence, did nothing to end the terribly oppressive institution of slavery.

The great freedom movement of the nineteenth century called abolitionism was also accompanied by much intolerance. Though the North generally opposed slavery and southern secession, its citizens prior to the Civil War often imposed harsh penalties on the radical speech of the abolitionists, many of whose homes and businesses were vandalized or burned as a result of the public discomfort caused by their reform zeal. And even though the radical Republicans in the North fought for equality and greater civil rights for blacks, they did nothing for the civil rights of women, who still could not even vote.

The period following the Civil War was a time of great freedom for American enterprise. Accompanying this freedom, however, was a corresponding oppression of the industrial workers. Those who advocated any assertion of working-class freedoms were either silenced or imprisoned, as happened with the Haymarket incident of 1886, where mass arrests occurred of workers striking a McCormick reaper factory. This accelerating power and consolidation of monopolistic trusts eventually brought about the populist movement – the first large-scale reform movement since the pre–Civil War period. Although the populists opposed the monopoly power of the increasingly concentrated industrial corporations and sought greater freedom for farmers and rural communities from dependence on the harsh economic power of the trusts, they also proved to be quite intolerant of immigrants, blacks, and civil liberties in general. Moreover, as religious traditionalists, they firmly opposed the growing secularism and freedom of modern society.

The progressive movement in the early twentieth century advocated social reform and particularly the freeing of children from oppressive working conditions. Yet it ignored the plight of Native Americans, who after Wounded Knee in 1890 had become an almost totally subjugated people. The progressives also virtually ignored the loss of democratic freedoms of southern blacks through voting restrictions and the fear of lynching. Indeed, the sufferings of Native and African-Americans were akin to the plight of immigrants in general, who came to the United States because of the promise of freedom, but often found it denied. To the Irish throughout the nineteenth century, signs of "No Irish Need Apply" frustrated their search for American opportunity. Thus, their search for freedom began with an experience of repression and rejection.

America's entry into World War I on the side of international democracy and freedom produced, unfortunately, a domestic assault against individual freedoms. During and after the war, and especially in the wake of the Bolshevik Revolution in Russia, the federal government used the Espionage and Sedition Acts of 1917 and 1918 to silence political dissidents. Those advocating pacifism, socialism, or anarchy were either harassed or arrested. In the Palmer raids of 1920, Federal authorities arrested more than four thousand supposed radicals on a single night. Immigrants from Russia who held radical beliefs were especially targeted for censure. This repression of dissident speech continued into the economic hard times of the 1930s, when labor unions tried to organize the nearly helpless work force. Many cities and states in the 1930s placed a total ban on labor organizing.

A similar reaction against freedom occurred in the wake of World War II and the triumph of the democratic allies. As the Cold War developed and the fear of Communist threat intensified, Senator Joseph McCarthy's "Red hunt" exposed a nation willing to ignore violations of individual freedom because of the paranoid ravings of a demagogue. Congress passed a new round of laws aimed against Communist sympathizers and activists; and the House Un-American Activities Committee (HUAC) conducted an inquisition not only against any government officials suspected of "un-American" tendencies, but against Hollywood writers and directors who had expressed any radical beliefs or who had even once belonged to any leftist organizations.

Throughout its history, the Hollywood television and movie industry has continually faced censorship as it has pushed for greater public expression of new ideas. As American society developed new forms of, and opportunities for, expression throughout the twentieth century, it has also felt the restraining hand of censorship. The expansion of book publishing and readership in the 1920s brought a wave of book censorship. The emerging motion picture industry in the 1930s met the silencing force of censorship. So too was it with the developing industries of paperback books, magazines, television, and music recordings in the 1950s and 1960s.

The decade of the 1960s, with its unprecedented openness, naturally ushered in a new era of censorship. Occurrences of censorship began as a response to political speech, such as Sheriff Bull Connor's stifling of civil rights demonstrators in Alabama, but eventually spread to many other types of expression that challenged conventional beliefs. As experiments with greater freedom occurred in nearly every aspect of American life, and as many traditional restraints were thrown off, particularly through the sexual revolution, the push for censorship intensified. With various cultural and minority groups seeking recognition and parity within the social landscape, cultural and ethnic speech became politicized as never before.

Political protests and cultural radicalism tested the bounds of social permissiveness. The battle over freedom of speech symbolized the cultural battle over traditional values. As the personal became political, as in the area of sex, public speech became increasingly emotional and divisive. Drugs were endorsed as personal liberators, the flag was burned as a protest against the war, and sexual depictions in art and in the cinema became more explicit as expressions of a new sexual freedom. Indeed, the liberating events of the 1960s created the conditions for the increased censorship activity during the following decades and existing at the present time.

Following the expansion of freedoms in the 1960s, the 1970s witnessed a backlash of censorship. In a return to the practices of the 1920s, book-banning and book-burning occurred. The novel *Slaughterhouse-Five* was burned at Drake, North Dakota, in 1974. Other book burnings included *Of Mice and Men* at Oil City, Pennsylvania, and Simon, Howe, and Kirschenbaum's *Values Clarification* at Warsaw, Indiana, in 1977; a pile of books including *National Geographic, Daffy Duck,* and *Fifty True Tales of Terror* were burned at Omaha, Nebraska, in 1981; and *The Living Bible* went up in flames at Gastonia, North Carolina, in 1981.[11]

Although the writers of the 1960s had found a receptive audience in their radical and unconventional works, book-banning continued in the 1970s. Some of the books most frequently banned from schools included *The Autobiography of Malcolm X, Diary of a Young Girl, Custer Died for Your Sins: An Indian Manifesto, The Hobbit, Lady Chatterley's Lover, The Scarlet Letter, Soul on Ice, Catcher in the Rye, Catch-22, The Grapes of Wrath, To Kill a Mockingbird,* and *Of Mice and Men.*[12] Surprisingly, considering the sexual revolution of the 1960s, books on sex education were commonly banned. Such titles included *Anatomy of the Human Body, A Boy Today, A Man Tomorrow,*

How to Avoid Social Diseases: A Handbook, and *Sex in the Adolescent Years: New Directions in Teaching and Guiding Youth.*[13]

Researchers who have studied censorship during the 1970s have concluded that its occurrence continually increased during that decade.[14] Some also believe that many more unreported incidents of book-banning occurred.[15] Estimates indicate that such censorship increased even more during the 1980s.[16]

The history of American freedom and censorship demonstrates the intermingling of those movements throughout time. This history also demonstrates, however, that the cause of free expression generally prevails over the interests of censorship. Most speech censored in earlier times is now freely expressed without restraint. In this century alone, the Supreme Court has reversed itself several times on censorship. Contrary to earlier decisions, it has held that motion pictures qualify for First Amendment protections and that political sedition laws are unconstitutional. No longer can individuals be punished for expressing socialist or Communist ideas. Americans are not only free to criticize their political and economic system, they may even do so with language that is offensive and rude.

As American society has become more open, so too has its public expression on such topics as sex, morality, art, and cultural values. Indeed, contemporary society seems to thrive on intentionally shocking speech. The confrontational and controversial radio talk shows, tabloids, and music lyrics feed that thriving. Even the Reverend Al Sharpton, who frequently offends Jewish groups and interests, often attracts a large audience of Jews at his speeches. Yet despite this openness to speech and despite the failure of censorship at any point in history to achieve lasting success, it continues to surface in many forms in connection with many issues today.

This intermingling of censorship and freedom in American history makes it difficult to determine the causes of censorship. Of course, there are certain generally consistent features of censorship. Conservative religious groups have usually advocated censorship of expressions concerning sexual matters. Various kinds of speech and ideas deemed un-American have been censored at different times. And as mass media has so pervasively impacted society, there have been increasing concerns over the exposure of children to supposedly immoral and disturbing ideas.

The special role and nature of speech in the human condition also contributes to the censorship impulse. As communication is one of the most human of activities, people take a certain pride in the quality of that activity. Moreover, since speech defines and shapes the direction of society, like a lighthouse directing ships, a strong impulse exists to clean the lens of expression every now and then.

Despite the consistent concerns over the quality of our public speech, the particular causes of specific censorship campaigns are difficult to define. After all, members of an occupation most dedicated to the value and quality of speech – librarians – are also as a group most consistently opposed to any form of censorship. Further camouflaging the causes of censorship is the inconsistent identity of its advocates.

Not only is there no single consistent force behind censorship, there are also no historically consistent persons or groups that are responsible for censorship crusades. For instance, in the early 1830s, Andrew Jackson, who broadened the right to vote and eased property-ownership requirements on that right, tried to prohibit the mailing of abolitionist tracts into the South. Later, Abraham Lincoln came to the aid of abolitionists and blacks, yet he also approved of restrictions on those who opposed the war. President Woodrow Wilson led progressive reforms in the name of individual freedom and democracy, yet he acceded in wartime and postwartime restrictions on the right of free speech and association of socialists, radicals, and pacifists. His Attorney General, A. Mitchell Palmer, instigated the infamous Palmer raids against suspected political dissidents. And Franklin Roosevelt, despite all of his liberal programs of the New Deal, not only censored Japanese-Americans during the war but even confined them into relocation camps.

The pattern continues today. Religious groups that favor censorship of sexually explicit material oppose censorship of the teaching of creationism in the schools. Indeed, there currently exists both censorship by the Right, such as religious fundamentalists, and censorship by the Left, such as feminist and civil rights groups. Corporations try to stop censorship of advertising, yet often try to censor speech critical of the economic status quo. And liberal academics, who may favor the exclusion of politically incorrect speech from college campuses, oppose the censorship of radical political speech and secular humanism.

Contemporary censorship in the 1980s and 1990s, though emanating from a wide array of sources, nonetheless reflects certain recurrent themes. As reflected in popular music, censorship continues to be generational. Indeed, this aspect may even be intensifying, since speech may be the only way to separate or define the generations. In the past, the younger generation left home and followed the call to "go west." Travel restrictions then prevented any future mingling of generations. Yet today children are increasingly staying longer at their parents' home. Instead of leaving home, the youth are simply buying a stereo system.

Contemporary censorship also involves familiar topics, such as sex, violence, crime, and religion. Likewise, book-banning and movie censorship have continued to exist, although to differing degrees, through most of this century.[17] And censorship campaigns in education are nothing new – they date back at least to the highly visible 1925 Scopes trial, in which a high school science teacher who taught Darwin's evolution theory was tried for violating a Tennessee law forbidding public school instructors to teach the theory that humans had evolved from lower forms of life.

Contemporary censorship, however, does possess certain unique characteristics that differentiate it from censorship crusades in the past. The present period, though one of relatively more censorship than the 1960s, is nonetheless a time of less social turmoil and unrest. The early 1970s, for instance, witnessed efforts by the federal government to stop antiwar demonstrators in Washington. Yet without a similar crisis of national security existing at the present time, censorship continues to exist. Moreover, current censorship involves different kinds of speech – art funded by the NEA, commercial advertising of certain products, racial or ethnic hate speech, and even the novel *The Adventures of Huckleberry Finn*. The recent efforts of college administrators to promulgate codes that punish racist and other forms of hate speech, for instance, threaten to chill the type of vigorous campus debate that was fought for in the 1960s.

Unlike the censorship campaigns of the 1950s and 1960s, contemporary censorship does not emanate so singularly from religious groups seeking to maintain traditional values. Instead, various social interest groups advocate censorship as part of their political agenda. These activist interest groups have replaced the social and religious elite as sponsors and advocates of censorship. Furthermore, the diversity and multiculturalism of society have greatly increased the number of voices and the competition and conflict of ideas. This social conflict over cultural identity has spilled over into battles over censorship. Consequently, contemporary censorship appears to be a symptom of a widening, more diverse democracy with competing voices, rather than a result of a homogeneous elite attempting to maintain social control.

The unique and diverse patterns of contemporary censorship suggest that its causes are both varied and subtle. Since censorship has been a consistently recurrent social phenomenon, its causes lie deep in the social fabric. Along with the lesson of history, these deeply rooted causes suggest that censorship cannot be resolved or erased simply by opposing it or by setting the argument of freedom against it. Indeed, specific censorship attempts have almost always been defeated when they have finally reached the courts or come to a head in the political process. Yet the process of that defeat takes a long time. Meanwhile, the distraction and diversion of the censorship controversy absorb the national energy. Thus, because of this distractive power of censorship, its underlying social causes must be understood and addressed, not only for the sake of combating the dark side of censorship but also for the sake of the health and functioning of our democratic process.

Censorship battles tend to be particularly divisive and unproductive. As such, they divert the national attention from other pressing social matters. Perhaps this distractive effect arises because censorship issues tend to involve cultural or moral values that trigger human emotions. But perhaps it also arises because Americans are apparently becoming more thin-skinned. More people seem to be getting offended by what others say. Indeed, the monumental increase in libel and slander litigation suggests that people tend to be more offended by the verbal and written assaults of others.

This increasing sensitivity to speech has also exerted additional influences on the legal arena. For instance, the legal causes of action relating to speech have expanded beyond slander and libel to include invasion of privacy, defamation, infliction of emotional distress, harassment, and discrimination. In addition to legal actions over speech, a general concern for civility in speech has become especially pronounced. Censorship attempts have focused on trying to achieve a greater civility between diverse groups in society. Yet these attempts occur at a time when American society has become more civil than at any other time in history. No longer are derogatory sexist or racist terms commonly used in daily conversation, and the use of offensive words for various ethnic groups has greatly diminished.

Whatever the causes of this increased sensitivity to speech – and perhaps the cause stems from the censorship impulse in society – it contributes to the distractive power of censorship issues in a democratic society. To understand this distractive power is to further appreciate the need to come to terms with the social forces that propel censorship in the United States.

Censorship and the Distortion of American Politics

Censorship has been defeated many times. It was defeated in 1800 when Thomas Jefferson assumed the presidency and pardoned those who had been convicted under the Alien and Sedition Acts. It was defeated each time a literary work was removed from the list of the banned, when authors like James Joyce and D. H. Lawrence could see their books freely distributed. It was defeated with each court decision in the twentieth century in which official censorship measures were overturned. And censorship is defeated each time a local school board denies a request to remove a book from the school library or from the course curriculum, and each time Americans tolerate speech on matters disagreeable or distasteful to them.

Our society has come a long way from the early days of television and motion pictures, when censors or program sponsors strictly reviewed scripts for compliance with rigid standards of acceptable expressions. In the 1960s, for instance, several music groups that appeared on the "Ed Sullivan Show" had to change the lyrics of any song that might have offended or worried the producers, and the "Smothers Brothers Comedy Hour" was abruptly canceled because of its politically irreverent and critical content. Today, on the other hand, television programs often need to generate some controversy in order to stay on the air. And a constant challenge faced by contemporary music groups is to prevent their lyrics from becoming too bland.

Although censorship has been defeated many times in the past, it has never been resolved. For to resolve the occurrences of censorship, we must discover and address the social forces underlying censorship crusades. Yet society's primary focus on the question of censorship has usually occurred in the courts, which have to deal with the legal disputes over censorship activity of the government. The courts, however, can only tell the government how far it can go in controlling or interfering with whatever speech is at issue. They cannot determine the initial social and political causes of the eventual government censorship activity, nor can they resolve whatever underlying concerns the advocates for censorship may have been trying to address through censorship. The courts can only uphold or overturn each particular government-sanctioned censorship attempt.

Judicial determinations of specific censorship questions have often failed to resolve in the public mind the rules pertaining to that particular kind of censorship. For instance, the Supreme Court ruled in *Miller v. State of California* that certain obscene speech could be censored if "the average person applying contemporary community standards would find that the work taken as a whole appeals to the prurient interest."[1] Although this test was intended as an objective test, it is fraught with vague and uncertain elements and requirements. Thus, even if the public's censorship attitudes rested on the rulings of the Court, those rulings fail to provide sufficiently specific and objective standards on which the public can rely.

Two important reasons exist for why society should not look to the courts for a fundamental resolution of the censorship question. First, the courts can generally only entertain cases involving government censorship – that is, where some governmental act or regulation infringes or restrains speech. However, since much censorship activity in society takes place outside of any governmental agency or activity, as is particularly the case at the present time, the courts are excluded from a majority of censorship matters that arise. Second, the judicial system can address a censorship issue only long after the particular censorship activity has been in effect and has slowly proceeded through the legal process to a final resolution. Because of the long delays in the judicial process, the courts often cannot aid the public in resolving or avoiding protracted and divisive censorship conflicts that absorb its social and political energies.

This distractive quality of censorship presents one of its greatest dangers. As history has revealed, censorship of particular expressions never endures – the marketplace of ideas is never fully and forever denied the censored speech. Eventually, repressed speech breaks out into unfettered expression. However, the time and energy that society expends in the fight over censorship can never be regained. The more

America concentrates its political and social energy on censorship matters, the less attention democratic politics can devote to the more pressing issues of the time. Consequently, politics becomes less responsive to the real needs of society. Thus, not only does our preoccupation with censorship prevent us from addressing other social concerns that require action, but it also contributes to a politics in which both public trust and political efficiency are eroded.

The distractive power of censorship arises in part from the democratic mindset. Democracy requires public attention on public issues. However, the framers of American democracy devised a political system subordinate to society and thus forced to compete with other social concerns for the attentions of the citizenry. Within the scheme of America's constitutional democracy, the government and political system were to be limited. Consequently, in the American democratic tradition, individuals have generally possessed and exercised a limited amount of political energy and attention. This limited political attention is reflected in the part-time status of many state legislatures.

As a democracy ultimately run by citizens concerned with private careers, family lives, and community activities, America is capable of devoting only so much of its attention to the political arena. The more attention siphoned off by censorship battles, the less that is available for perhaps more pressing commitments. Thus the distractive role: an overly extended emphasis on censorship issues distracts the nation from needed action on other political matters.

It is difficult to determine how much of society's attention and energy are devoted toward censorship disputes. Censorship has existed in various forms throughout the nation's history, and therefore we cannot precisely determine the amount of social energy devoted to censorship simply through the presence of such issues. Nonetheless, one rough indication of the social energy consumed by censorship is the amount of attention devoted to such issues in the national political arena.

Throughout this century, a historical correlation has occurred between activity on censorship issues and inactivity on other social and political matters. In the 1920s, in the aftermath of World War I and the progressive reform movement, a great deal of censorship by the government took place — in the form of book seizures and arrests of radicals suspected of socialist or Communist sympathies. In 1930, the United States Senate devoted an unprecedented four days of debate to a federal censorship program. At the same time, very little action took place on social problems.

The 1950s were another period of relative political inaction on domestic social issues, but it was a period of much censorship activity. In addition to the government's involvement in McCarthyism, there existed much censorship activity by religious groups that went unchallenged in the courts.[2] During the 1950s, extensive censorship pressures played on the television, film, and movie industries.

The 1980s was another period of heavy censorship activity and relatively little political action on the nation's social problems. Obscenity prosecutions doubled from 1987 to 1988, and then quadrupled from 1988 to 1989. Throughout the decade, Congress considered bills that would regulate the content of television programming. In fact, in 1991 a federal court overturned an FCC regulation imposing a twenty-four-hour ban on indecent programming on television and radio. Of course, significant political attention during the decade was riveted on such matters as flag-burning and funding of the NEA. Even the presidential campaign of 1988 focused on a censorship issue: whether the state should mandate the recitation of the Pledge of Allegiance.

The recurrence of censorship issues in the political arena has necessarily occupied and diverted the legislative attentions of Congress. Consider, for instance, the legislative energies devoted to censorship during the decade of the 1960s. In 1967, forty-three bills dealing with obscenity were introduced in Congress. During that same year, in response to court decisions overturning various censorship attempts, Congress created the Commission on Obscenity and Pornography to study the causal relationship between sexually oriented materials and antisocial behavior. The commission's findings, in turn, were hotly and heavily debated by legislators and politicians. Two years earlier, twenty-one obscenity-related bills had been introduced, as well as more than twenty other bills dealing with various other aspects of censorship. In 1963, nineteen obscenity bills were introduced. The previous year, forty-eight speeches on the floor of Congress addressed censorship. And twenty-seven obscenity bills were considered by Congress in 1961.

Censorship issues have therefore greatly absorbed the energies of our political system. Because of this diversion of attentions, the institutions of government have often been preoccupied with the recurrent problem of censorship. This preoccupation in turn has contributed to the inability to sufficiently concentrate on more immediate problem areas such as education, drug abuse, child welfare, crime, and environmental pollution. Moreover, even if censorship issues do not end up in the courts or legislatures, as they commonly do not, these issues still occupy a great deal of public attention. This is evident in the current wave of censorship activity. Indeed, the Office for Intellectual Freedom of the American Library Association found that censorship attempts tripled during the period 1975 to 1979, and tripled again during the first half of the decade of the 1980s.[3] Another indication of the increasing attention devoted to censorship is the number of articles in professional journals dealing with the topic. According to one count, 871 articles were written between 1940 and 1949, 1,544 articles were published during the next decade, 2,787 articles appeared from 1960 to 1969, and 3,876 were written during the decade ending in 1980.[4]

All of this attention, however, has failed to diminish the censorship impulse. The speech being censored today, for instance, is similar in many ways to the speech that was being censored half a century ago. As in the 1920s and 1930s, we are still trying to censor sex. Obviously, we have not come to terms with whether and how much we should allow public expression regarding certain matters involving sex.

We are also still divided on how much information we should trust to the schools to impart to our children. The Scopes trial in 1925, for instance, involved the question of whether evolution could be taught in the public schools. Today, we continue to debate that issue, and we have added another twist. Not only are religious fundamentalists opposing the teaching of evolution, as they did in the Scopes trial, but they are also advocating the elimination of secular humanism from the curriculum. Not until 1990 did the Texas Board of Education, for instance, fully approve of textbooks that discussed the theory of evolution.

In education in general, like generations past, we are still exerting heavy censorship of what our children read and see. Within the last year, books including *The Adventures of Tom Sawyer* and *The Adventures of Huckleberry Finn, The Catcher in the Rye, The Grapes of Wrath* and *Ulysses* were banned or removed from school libraries. Even *My Friend Flicka* was removed from a sixth-grade reading list in Green Cove Springs, Florida, because the book contained the words "damn" twice and "bitch" once. A Mankato, Minnesota, school system excluded books advocating corporal punishment, and in the state of California during a recent two-year period there were approximately three hundred censorship challenges to various books, films, and other school materials used in the education curriculum. About half of those challenges were based on religious grounds or on objections to depictions of Satan or witchcraft included in such classics as Shakespeare's *Macbeth* and even in *Snow White*. Even films such as *E.T.* met with censorship challenges.

Sexually provocative and explicit materials continue to endure censorship pressures, as they have since public reactions against such classic literature as Nabokov's *Lolita*, Joyce's *Ulysses*, and Lawrence's *Women in Love*. Today, as in the 1960s and 1970s, groups ranging from religious fundamentalists to radical feminists oppose the distribution and content of magazines like *Playboy* and *Penthouse*. As with the play *Oh, Calcutta!* in the 1960s, controversial plays and movies still feel the threat of censorship. The play, *Norman, Is That You?*, was canceled from various performances across the state of Florida. It is a comedy about a couple who discover their son is gay. The cancellations, according to gay rights activists, were part of a statewide censorship craze.

In the music field, things may not have changed greatly since Elvis

Presley first came on the scene. Just as many found Elvis's gyrating pelvis in need of censorship, so too do many find Madonna's lyrics and antics similarly worthy of censorship. And as 1960s rock groups like The Doors, Frank Zappa, and The Rolling Stones irritated the censorship nerve, so too do contemporary groups like 2 Live Crew and The Dead Kennedys.

Thus, the censorship questions of the last three or four decades have continued to recur and distract American society. Issues of free expression that we thought were settled in the 1960s and 1970s remain with us in the 1980s and 1990s. Though other political issues like budget deficits and crime control persistently remain on the public agenda, unlike censorship issues they do not absorb an inordinately large amount of social attention and energy. In fact, the current complaint is that censorship issues command too little attention. In a recent *New York Times* poll, the respondents named morality and pornography as more important problems facing the nation than those surrounding the savings and loan bailout, child abuse, women's issues, Soviet relations, family breakdown, and Japanese competition.[5]

The attention-absorbing power of censorship and its consequent distractive role derive from the public's tendency to take an immediate interest in censorship matters and to become quickly opinionated on those matters. Unlike complicated budget and foreign policy issues, questions on censorship can be easily understood and lend themselves to rather quick and definite judgments. As the opinion polls demonstrate, few people fail to form an opinion on censorship issues in the political arena, such as flag-burning and the funding of the NEA. Polls conducted in 1990 on the flag-burning issue, for instance, revealed that only 5 percent of the people surveyed had failed to form an opinion on the issue.[6] On the other hand, polling on such issues as the environment, education policy, and the savings and loan crisis produced "no opinion" responses from up to 20 percent of the respondents.[7]

Public opinion tends to be much more flexible or uncertain on issues that are complex or involve judgments on highly specialized information. Government economic programs such as the agricultural program, for instance, are so complex and specialized that few persons understand them. Consequently, only a small segment of the public not actually involved in a program forms specific and firm opinions about it. Censorship issues, on the other hand, do not involve such highly specialized knowledge or information. They do not involve government programs evolving over decades of political existence. Instead, people can form an opinion on these issues by glancing at the newspaper headlines while drinking a cup of coffee.

Language is one of the few identifying characteristics of a nation and society. As such, it is often an emotive issue. This emotion is seen in countries where, for instance, two or more languages compete for the national identity. Confusion, anger, violence, and separatist movements have characterized the struggles between English-speaking and French-speaking Canada. Differences simply in language, not to mention content of that language, often inspire emotional reactions. Even the regional differences in American speech tend to prompt emotional responses among persons of different speech groups – Northern, Midland, Southern, and New England.[8]

Thus, judgments on censorship issues tend to be formed rather quickly and rather strongly. There is usually no factual research or additional knowledge needed for an individual to form a judgment on such issues. Indeed, very few people proceed to the more abstract and objective question of whether a free society ought to allow a particular repulsive speech. Yet even consideration of this question need not preclude the formation of a strong opinion, since most persons have some concept of freedom that would enable them to reach a fairly definite opinion.

As a result of censorship issues quickly galvanizing public opinion, political battles relating to these issues also tend to become particularly fierce and protracted. Debate does little to change minds. Opinions run high and intense, and the political process tends to become a bitter fight rather than a process of resolution. Consider, for example, the intense and dragged-out debates over the various legislative proposals introduced in 1990 in connection with funding of the NEA and possible restrictions on the types of art funded by the agency. Although a bipartisan commission had been created by Congress to review the NEA's grant-making procedures, a political impasse and stalemate still occurred in Congress because of wide disagreement over how to handle the agency and the art that it funds. This impasse obviously devoured much of Congress's legislative energies.

As demonstrated by this NEA struggle, inordinately large amounts of energy are consumed in dealing with censorship disputes. This diversion of political energy also results from the emotional nature of censorship matters. Although, as earlier mentioned, speech can carry emotive power in itself, the particular speech that becomes the object of censorship attempts is often speech relating to an especially emotional issue for Americans.

Censorship issues tend to be some of the most emotional issues in the public arena. Not only does it touch upon an activity that lies at the heart of human freedom and that expresses the most personal of all human possessions – thoughts and feelings – censorship also often tends to occur with speech about moral and cultural issues. These issues evoke strong and passionate emotions and can be highly divisive. Consider, for instance, the abortion issue – obviously a very emotional one. Censorship has been frequently attempted on this issue by groups on both sides of the debate. The most recent examples of censorship of abortion-related speech include, by the prolife faction, a federal regulation prohibiting clinics receiving federal funds from even mentioning abortion, and, by the prochoice side, the attempts to ban or restrict the picketing of prolifers outside abortion clinics. Thus, the emotional nature of abortion, as demonstrated by its political history throughout the last two decades, clearly contributes to the distractive power of censorship issues relating to expression of abortion views.

The emotional aspect, and hence distractive power, of censorship also arises from the symbolic nature of speech. When a person burns a flag on national television, he or she is not perceived to be simply performing an isolated individual act. Instead, at issue is the symbol of a community, a nation, and perhaps even a way of life or a set of values. Consequently, such an act inspires emotional reactions in each person who witnesses it through the media, primarily because of the emotional feeling about that which the flag symbolizes. A similar reaction occurs with racist or pornographic speech. Such speech becomes a symbol for the type of society in which the speech is made. When we hear racist speech, a desire for censorship may run high from the symbolism created—since symbols often define society, symbols of racism may denote a racist society.

As a symbol, speech can epitomize or even become the reality surrogate of personal beliefs and values. Expressions about sex, for instance, can become emotionally and even logically the act about which one speaks. Thus, if a person thinks a certain sexual act is morally wrong, any expressions about that act can also be morally wrong. Though it is a product of a logical language system and a cognitive reasoning process, speech nonetheless carries great emotional intensity as it touches the human soul and heart, as well as the mind. And when speech occurs on value-laden or personal issues, the response to that speech will be highly emotional. Moreover, it need hardly be said that emotional matters absorb and consume our attentions and energies more than more unemotional ones.

Consequently, when censorship conflicts enter the political forum, they often become intensely emotional. As a result, the political system bogs down in divisiveness. Reflecting the emotions of the individuals participating in it, politics becomes emotional in itself. More passionate speeches are made, and even more emotions are aroused. In the recent NEA funding debate, for instance, Congress went into great detail about what kind of art the agency should fund. With no other agency does Congress try to monitor and control so closely the daily workings and operation. Yet while the economy continued to lumber under the budget deficit and children went hungry and uneducated, Congress devoted days and weeks talking about art. Because of the symbolic, emotional nature of the issue, however, Congress was not only talking about art, it was discussing national values and identity.

Symbolic and emotional issues like censorship have played an increasingly distractive role in modern American politics. During the last several years, the great ideological battles have shifted from the field of economics to that of culture. Controversies over free speech and the arts, multiculturalism and education, and the relations between races and genders have stirred more intense passions than have any disputes over economic policy or electoral politics.

E. J. Dionne argues in *Why Americans Hate Politics* that our political leaders have allowed politics to be dominated by symbolic issues that have little practical or social relevance. For instance, instead of dealing with the causes of crime, politicians simply debate the symbolic and largely ineffectual death penalty. As Dionne recognizes, symbolic issues tend to be highly emotional and tend to distract the political system from other more relevant and urgent issues.

Like the death penalty, abortion is also, in part, a symbolic issue. Compared with issues of child care and education, it exerts little practical influence on the daily family life of most Americans. Yet it has consumed a disproportionate share of political attention in recent decades and has caused great divisiveness in the political process. Abortion has not only inspired intense passions, but also produced rigid positions on each side of the issue. In 1988, only 2 percent of the population had no opinion on the question of legality of abortion, and when asked if the advanced medical knowledge gained over the last decade about the first stages of life had changed their opinion, more than 70 percent responded in the negative.[9] Though the rigidity and influence of such issues as abortion may be a handicap of the political system, it also is a problem of censorship, since it is one of the more emotional issues that cause similar distractions to society.

The distractive effect of censorship further elevates the need to discover and resolve the underlying causes and motivations for censorship. The challenge is to resolve censorship in a manner that will lessen its occurrence and its consequent distractive power. We must attempt to go beyond simply waging the censorship war—fighting over whether censorship should occur every time controversial expressions take place. History demonstrates that no matter how many times censorship is defeated, it continues to return. And if the recent decade is any indication, censorship attempts are not only persisting, but increasing.

Since censorship has never been resolved, in the sense that its social foundations have not been discovered and addressed, it has had a snowball or cumulative effect over time. Even though particular censorship attempts, such as those dealing with flag desecration and sexually explicit expressions, may fail on a regular basis, they contribute to a snowball effect insofar as they continually recur and their underlying causes remain unaddressed. As society becomes increasingly familiar and comfortable with censorship, the recurrent pattern of censorship is further solidified.

Court judgments on censorship disputes have not fundamentally resolved the public's concerns or censorship desires. For decades the judiciary has handled censorship cases involving sexual and political discussion. In the 1950s, the courts addressed censorship of ideas perceived to be un-American, while in the 1980s the courts addressed censorship of supposedly un-American activities like flag-burning. And throughout the last four decades, the courts have tried to draw the line between protected sexual speech and constitutionally unprotected obscenity. Yet despite the volume of case law, censorship attempts keep surfacing in the public—a public whose attitudes and concerns underlying and motivating its censorship impulse have not been settled by any court decree.

The snowball effect of recurrent censorship also endangers the growth and development of the new communications technologies emerging today. The introduction of new forms of media and communications services has historically been accompanied by a wave of censorship aimed at that new media form. When motion pictures were introduced, they inspired intense censorship activity. Books, which had been the previous subject of censorship, suddenly were significantly more free of such pressures. When magazines and paperbacks became popular in the 1950s, censorship advocates immediately turned to these forms. Television and record albums in turn became the censors' targets in the 1960s and 1970s. The recent introduction of computer information systems, electronic mail, computer bulletin boards, and telecommunication services like the 900 system promise to greatly expand the individual's ability to communicate personally with a greater number and diversity of people. Not surprisingly, however, these new media and communications technologies are being met with censorship pressures. If censorship is to be kept from suffocating these new communications services before they can fully develop, as it almost did with the motion picture industry in the 1930s, the snowball effect of the censorship impulse in society must be lessened. Otherwise, censorship attempts in the future will be more intense and will have deeper social roots, and will thus be harder to defeat. Furthermore, the snowball effect will propagate the illusory influence of censorship.

Censorship often creates the illusion that a social problem has disappeared if the speech highlighting that problem has disappeared. However, just because a child quits complaining about vegetables does not mean that she is going to eat them. Likewise, just because the social dialogue contains fewer references to violence or AIDS does not mean that those problems have diminished, particularly if the decline in speech about those problems results from censorship pressures.

The human tendency, of course, is to try to eradicate the appearance of a problem, especially if the problem itself cannot be easily remedied. That is why parental demands for clean rooms often translate into a more compact but hidden mess under the bed. Just as the progressive social reform movement of the early twentieth century initially sought to clean up society and ended up trying to clean up the books that society read, activists today who want to stop alcohol and tobacco abuse or who want to fight racism frequently end up trying to censor the speech signifying those problems.

Censorship offers an easy way to substitute quality of life concerns for quality of speech concerns. Particularly in our modern media society, we tend to think that if the problem is not talked about or depicted on the television, it has gone away. But if censorship is used to achieve this illusion, it has given a false sense of security – a false security that must be maintained through increased censorship in the future. Consequently, we become more and more dependent on censorship.

Only by confronting truth through open and free discussion can this snowball effect of censorship be reduced. The desire for truth has often proved an effective censorship repellent. Since the pursuit of truth is the first step to meaningful action, a close tie exists between speech, truth, and action. If we censor our speech, we tie our hands from action and close our mind to truth. Senator Bill Bradley recognized this need for open dialogue in a recent speech on race relations.[10] He warned that our unwillingness to speak straightforwardly about race only causes the underlying race problems to continue simmering. In warning against our self-imposed censorship on such sensitive and emotional issues, Senator Bradley stated that "we will never understand the problems of our cities until a white person can point out the epidemic of minority illegitimacy, drug addiction and homicides without being charged a racist." Indeed, the desire for truth and for action greatly influences the American attitudes toward speech and censorship.

As Justice Oliver Wendell Holmes stated in his 1919 dissent in *Abrams v. United States,* speech in America deserves protection and freedom because only through the competition of free and unhindered speech can society discover the truth necessary to govern itself as a democracy. Since the people in a democratic society are the ultimate arbiters of social truth, there must exist a means by which the public can learn and acquire truth. As Justice Holmes stated, and as judges and philosophers since have recognized, the best and perhaps only means to acquire such truth is through open and free expression of ideas. Constitutional protections of free speech in the twentieth century have derived in large part from the American conception of democratic truth as the result of the free competition of ideas. Therefore, it is logical that censorship attitudes likewise derive from the underlying social attitudes toward truth.

The next chapter discusses contemporary American views and treatments of truth and how they affect attitudes toward censorship. If Americans view social and political truth in a way that puts fewer negative connotations on censorship, it is safe to assume that the public will more readily advocate censorship. Thus, although current censorship crusades may specifically focus on racist or sexual speech, they may in part be fueled by a particular conception of and attitude toward truth.

4

Truth Is No Longer a Defense

Truth can be like love. To define it, one must travel into the abstract realm of the philosophical. Yet even without a philosophical definition, we all want it in our daily lives and seem to instinctively know it when we have it.

Ideas, then, are like marriage. One is used to express truth, the other to express love. And just as our views on love directly influence our attitudes toward marriage, our view of truth affects our disposition toward the free expression or censorship of ideas.

The American view of free speech has always been intimately connected with its attitude toward social truth. Of course, there are many kinds of truth – some with lesser connections to free speech. There is scientific truth – the kind usually pursued in the laboratory. There is spiritual truth – the kind often sought through religion. And there is individual truth – the kind obtained through philosophy and life experience. Social truth, on the other hand, is the kind of truth on which our social systems and institutions are built. It is the type of truth, or consensus, that democratic societies must arrive at so as to govern and maintain themselves.

Democratic societies seek social truth through the process of self-government to construct a healthy society and to address social problems. Social truth, for example, shows society how to construct an efficient and equitable health care system, how to direct a proper foreign policy, or how to solve the problem of unemployment. Unlike eternal truth, which only a human being can know and which relates to the meaning of human life, social truth is not absolute and unchanging. Indeed, it can, and often does, change as knowledge expands and as new ideas are debated. Yet social truth does signify a somewhat permanent decision or judgment reached by society on a matter of public concern.

Social truth comprises the knowledge and judgments a society uses to make social policy. In a democratic society, it is the decisions the electorate and its representatives make and rely upon in conducting political governance. Since the people hold the ultimate political power in a democracy, social truth must come from them and rest with them.

When America became a nation and formed its political institutions, this conception of social truth was a radical idea. In the aristocratic societies of the rest of the world, the common person had nothing to do with realizing or determining social truth. Such a responsibility and privilege lay exclusively with the aristocratic class. Given the inherent privileged status conferred upon them at birth, the aristocratic rulers were the only ones deemed capable of determining social truth and governing society. These rulers consisted of the landed nobility and the religious authorities. Together they convinced the larger population that God had entrusted only them with the knowledge and use of truth.

Even today, many societies do not entrust the mass of their population with determining social truth. The few remaining Communist nations dictate social truth from the closed rooms of their totalitarian rulers. And religiously directed societies, such as Iran, grant to their religious leaders the power to know and dictate truth for the whole of society. However, as a democratic, nonsectarian nation, America must trust its citizen public with determining the social truths that will govern and guide the country.

Conferring upon the general public the power of social truth obviously requires some scheme or system to assist it in determining such truth. In America, this system is free expression. Through the free competition of ideas in the marketplace of communication, social truth will hopefully prevail and ultimately gain acceptance.

This role of free speech in the pursuit of truth was firmly recognized in Enlightenment political thought for more than a century preceding America's birth. After the adoption of the Bill of Rights, John Stuart Mill defended free speech when he wrote in *On Liberty* that truth is best attained when all ideas freely compete against each other through expression in the marketplace.[1] Significantly, Mill did not advocate free expression for any intrinsic value; instead, he advocated it as the best means for society to achieve the fundamental goal of truth. Mill's marketplace concept subsequently and significantly influenced the American development of basic free speech beliefs.[2]

American proponents of free expression at the time of the ratification of the Bill of Rights similarly believed that the value of uninhibited expression lay in the discovery of truth and in its contribution to the progress of humanity.[3] The Continental Congress continually expressed this conviction throughout the almost two-decade span preceding the adoption of the First Amendment. In its address to the people of Quebec, for instance, the Continental Congress advocated freedom of speech on the ground that it promotes truth.[4] Indeed, the United States' constitutional scheme rests on the belief that no single individual or group has a monopoly on the truth and that a free exchange of ideas offers the only path to social truth.

Twentieth-century theorists have continued to advocate the value of free expression in determining social truth. Professor Zecchariah Chafee concluded that "one of the most important purposes of society and government is the discovery and spread of truth on subjects of general concern, [and that] this is possible only through absolutely unlimited discussion."[5] Similarly, another widely respected free speech scholar, Alexander Meiklejohn, argued that the framers enacted the constitutional protection of speech to ensure the dissemination of the kind of political truth required for reasoned self-government.[6]

The truth value of free expression has held a prominent role in constitutional law since Justice Holmes first articulated it in his famous dissent in *Abrams v. United States*. Holmes opposed the censorship of radical speech in that case because, as he reasoned, "the best test of truth is the power of thought to get itself accepted in the competition of the market."[7] Subsequently, in *Whitney v. California*, Justice Louis Brandeis similarly stated that the First Amendment carries the assumption that free expression is indispensable to the "discovery and spread of political truth."[8] And in *United States v. Associated Press*, Judge Learned Hand endorsed the constitutional view that truth emerges in a free marketplace of ideas: "[The First Amendment] presupposes that right conclusions are more likely to be gathered out of a multitude of tongues, than through any kind of authoritative selection. To many, this is, and will always be folly; but we have staked our all on it."[9]

Thus, for nearly three centuries in America, the attainment of social and political truth has been intimately linked with free and uninhibited speech. Indeed, the modern constitutional protections for speech have derived from an understanding that social truth would be unattainable without a system of free expression. American constitutional history also shows that the more society values truth, the more it strives to protect the freedom of all speech. Consequently, the more America values truth and seeks to acquire it, the less tolerant it will be of censorship.

Since the nation's birth, Americans have generally believed that their nation was founded on and dedicated to truth. Compared with their old homelands, the America the immigrants came to know was a land where truth, not rigid and inherited social rules or class structures, would prevail and govern. Neither religious rules nor feudal caste systems would control their lives. Instead, the political and social life of the nation would be based on rationally determined objective truth. Eventually, the country came to be popularly symbolized by its adherence to "truth, justice, and the American way."

Because of its egalitarian society with political power resting in the individual, America developed a particular philosophy toward social truth. This philosophy was called pragmatism, and it especially fit the American experience. As the only democratic nation on earth, it had no blueprint for survival or success. The new nation had to make it on its own. And as a nation of immigrants from diverse cultures, there were relatively few social or cultural guidelines or rules. Finally, as a nation with a creed and belief in individualism and localism, there was no central authority directing the life of the country. America, essentially, had to chart its course as it went along. For this task, a pragmatic social philosophy was well suited.

Pragmatism reflected a belief in action and experience. It was not a philosophy based on theoretical abstractions, as were the philosophical orientations of Europe. To the pragmatists, what was true was what worked. Thus, pragmatism was appropriate for a nation that had to develop its own system of political governance and social truth.

Having broken from the philosophical orientation of Europe with the war for independence, America had to create its own philosophy. Not confined to ideological rigidities, pragmatism sought to discover objective truth through experience. Thus, the pragmatic method was a way to settle the ideological disputes that were engulfing European dialogue and that might otherwise go on forever. Similar to the American experience itself, pragmatism was not concerned with proving or supporting a particular definition of truth; it was concerned with discovering objective truth. Because, to pragmatists, the truth was what worked. Consequently, truth became a process of discovery, not an ideological orientation.

The American revolution had rejected the old political rules and wisdom of an age past. Likewise, pragmatism preached an open mind and rejection of all dogmas inherited from the past. This rejection, of course, required a replacement – and that replacement would be truth reached in a democratic manner. New truths would have to get themselves accepted in the marketplace of free speech. Thus, for the sake of determining social truth, a society had to avoid the censoring of different viewpoints. Because of this unique notion of truth, free speech became a right protected more in America than anywhere else in the world.

Not surprisingly, the American view of truth has changed somewhat over the last two centuries. However, perhaps the most dramatic change has occurred during the last several decades. This change consequently has produced changes in the American attitude toward censorship.

Under the early American pragmatism, truth was not a political concept or consequence; rather, politics depended on truth and strove to reflect and incorporate truth. But the early American political thinkers did not envision the evolution of the highly partisan political system existing now. Subsequently and more recently, however, another change occurred. In the last several decades, American politics has become increasingly ideological as well as more partisan. This partisan and ideological evolution of politics has replaced the role and influence of pragmatism. Thus, the pragmatic searching for objective truth has been increasingly subdued by the ideological orientation and evolution of America's political system.

The contemporary American attitude toward truth differs markedly, therefore, from the pragmatic outlook. Partisan and ideological combat has pushed aside a pursuit of objective truth, and political power has replaced free speech as the path to the desired goal. With truth becoming more of a social battleground, the outcome sought by the combatants is victory more than knowledge; and the forces are political power rather than rational persuasion.

The ideological orientation of American politics and social thought has also greatly inhibited consensus on public issues. In effect, the search for truth has been surrendered for the sake of ideological purity. Even when the factual evidence seems incontrovertible that certain social problems exist, ideological beliefs suggest that it is more important to remain ideologically consistent than to reach a pragmatic solution to the problem.

Truth today seems anything but objective and concrete, as the pragmatists envisioned. Rather, it seems vague, relative, and elusive. Perhaps this elusiveness results from the difficulty in sifting through all the knowledge and information that contemporary society has at its disposal. Indeed, society sometimes seems drowned in information.

Ideology often helps categorize and deal with all of this information and knowledge, usually by rejecting all information not supportive of a particular ideological orientation. Unfortunately, however, truth is something deeper than information and knowledge. Truth involves judgments and opinions on information.

Clearly, information alone does not yield truth. Take, for instance, the matter of health care. For two or three decades, the press has published in-depth accounts of the problems of the current health care system and formulations of various remedies or alternatives. Yet the public is nowhere nearer any conception of what to do about the system. There has been no achievement of any social judgment or determination of social truth on this matter. Despite the flood of information on the problem, no vision of social truth has emerged.

What has also clouded the American vision of truth has been the prevalence of a one-sided view of social truth. During the 1980s, Americans came to believe that if they tried hard enough, only one type of truth would exist – the pleasant type. Unpleasant truth could be wished away, or at least not accepted. Consequently, the public refused to accept the unpleasant truth about the budget deficits and the inevitable consequences of cutting taxes without decreasing expenditures. And with the debate over the NEA, the public tried to wipe out any kind of unpleasant or distasteful art.

As the current American attitude or treatment of truth has drifted away from a pragmatic view, attitudes toward free expression and censorship have also changed. With truth seen as a contest of competing ideological forces, censorship as an exercise of one of those forces can actually be seen as a route to truth. Thus, the decline in popularity of the view that differing speech must compete in the marketplace so that objective truth can emerge has obvious implications for freedoms of speech. Because in the past, the respect for truth has provided a defense to censorship attempts.

The social treatment of and attitudes toward truth consequently exert a significant impact on society's willingness to sponsor or tolerate censorship campaigns. These attitudes are reflected in various social institutions concerned with the treatment and pursuit of truth, including the nation's judicial, political, and educational systems. Therefore, to more fully understand how truth is treated in contemporary America and consequently how a diminished value of truth may result in a greater social propensity to censor, it is helpful to examine those systems and their treatment of truth.

TRUTH AND THE JUDICIAL SYSTEM

The role and treatment of truth in the judicial system reflects a certain cavalier or cynical attitude. In the trial process, truth is rarely given top priority. Instead, it is relegated to a hoped-for byproduct of an adversarial combat between litigants.

Trials have been commonly depicted as the public's way of finding out what happened in a disputed situation. At the start of most mystery novels or movies, the puzzle is presented: Who did it? What really happened? We do not really find out until the end, until a trial has taken place that reveals the facts. On the long-running television series "Perry Mason," the trial always produced the answers. Indeed, the courtroom seemed to be the one social institution in which the truth would always emerge.

Unfortunately, in the real world trials and truth are not always synonymous. That realization has caught on in many contemporary movies involving trials of a main character. In *Jagged Edge, Presumed Innocent,* and *An Innocent Man,* the trials did not reveal the truth; in fact, the truth was not revealed until after conclusion of the trial. These movies suggest what is becoming apparent: that the judicial system is not necessarily the reliable producer of truth that Perry Mason led us to believe it was.

The judicial system in the United States is an adversarial system. In such a system, determining the truth is not a direct or constant focus. Instead, it is an indirect or secondary goal that the courts hope to fulfill through the workings of the adversary system. Rather than truth, the judicial process focuses primarily on the rights of the participants. It is a rights-oriented process, not an outcome-oriented one. Participants are responsible only for what they can prove in their favor, not for revealing the truth.

Out of the combat of the participants, it is hoped that truth will somehow prevail. Yet because the courts' main focus is on following procedural rules rather than on independently discovering the truth, the role of truth in the legal process becomes relative and ambiguous. It depends on the perspective of the parties and their lawyers, the context in which the evidence is presented, and the credibility of the witnesses or parties. The jury, which must make the final determination of fact, sees only the evidence the parties choose to present and to which there are no successful legal objections. As passive spectators during the trial, the jurors cannot actively question the witnesses, the evidence, or the lawyers.

As all lawyers know, the jury rarely sees the whole picture. The lawyers and the judge prior to trial attempt to pare down the issues left to the jury and the evidence presented to it. For purposes of expediency and risk-avoidance, the jury is asked to render a decision on as few presented facts as possible. To the parties and their lawyers, the trial process is a contest that each side tries to win. To the judge, the trial is a process that seeks to reach an ultimate resolution of the dispute between the parties. It is only the jury that primarily seeks the truth. Yet that search is often frustrated by the adversary nature of the judicial process.

Several other aspects of the judicial process reveal its secondary treatment of truth. The rules of evidence, governing what can be presented to the jury, do not follow a free speech marketplace model but one of rigid censorship. Indeed, the rules specify countless types of evidence that cannot be presented, regardless of whether they might reflect the truth. Even if highly relevant, much hearsay evidence cannot be presented. Nor can certain evidence relating to a party's previous actions be presented. If a defendant, for instance, has been arrested for burglary once a year for the past ten years, that fact probably cannot be given to the jury in a trial for his most recent arrest for burglary. And the fact that a former cohort of the defendant was heard to say that the defendant committed the burglary also would most likely not be revealed.

The exclusionary rule also contradicts the interests of truth. This controversial rule prohibits the use at trial of any evidence the police improperly obtain during their investigation. For instance, if the police enter a person's home without a warrant and discover a murder weapon, they generally cannot present that evidence at trial. The exclusionary rule is intended to deter the police from violating constitutional rights of the individual. Yet instead of punishing the police, the rule punishes the truth. An overreaching police department receives no direct punishment, a potentially guilty criminal defendant goes free, and justice for the particular crime is left unserved. If truth were given a higher priority, perhaps the penalty against the police would be a suspension or termination of the offending officers – a sanction that would probably have a greater deterrent effect.

Another example of a truth-contradictory aspect of the adversarial judicial process involves the absence of any obligation of lawyers, who are officers of the court, to present the whole story. At trial, the lawyer has no duty to present facts that directly contradict her case, even if she possesses knowledge of those facts. Although the lawyer must not knowingly present false evidence, she is under no obligation to present all the true evidence she may possess. She needs only to present evidence that favors her client. If the other side does not possess these other facts, the jury will never hear them. Though lawyers may be officers of the court, they are not representatives of truth. Truth is not their client. As good lawyers know, the best trial defense is a good story, whether or not it is true – and indeed many lawyers do not want to know if it is true. This elasticity of courtroom truth is called advocacy by the legal profession.

Plea-bargaining is another judicial equivocation with the truth. In reality it is a negotiation with the truth. A person charged with a crime pleads guilty to some lesser crime. The state saves the money that a trial would cost and the possible embarrassment of a loss. The defendant receives a lesser penalty than would have been given if he were convicted at trial. Yet, as many investigative reports have shown, some defendants have pled guilty because they believed they would end up spending less time in prison than if they actually waited for a trial. And as the Wall Street insider-trading defendants like Dennis Levine and Michael Milken demonstrate, people can plead guilty and then claim that they never really did anything wrong, but could not afford to litigate against the powerful prosecution. In the midst of this process, truth disappears.

Trials have thus become battles and contests rather than discoverers of truth. After a famous trial ends, the lawyers write their books telling the public what really happened. Indeed, the public seems increasingly to be sensing that trials do not necessarily reveal the truth. Contemporary novels and movies seem to withhold the truth from revelation at trial. On "L.A. Law," for instance, the viewer rarely discovers the truth behind the trial, just the outcome of the trial and the agonizing of the lawyers. Even the trials that take place in real life seem to be so confusing that the public can never grasp the truth. Consider the example of Oliver North. After a long trial, the jury convicted him on several charges and acquitted him on others. Yet later on appeal the court dismissed the conviction, even though North admitted misleading Congress. So what did ever happen in the Iran-Contra affair? The public has little idea of the truth and even of whether the judicial system is able to somehow arrive at the truth.

This adversarial nature of the judicial process and its apparent lack of concern for the truth does not escape the attention of the public. Consequently, the judicial institution becomes less supportive of the social truth-finding process and even sometimes becomes antagonistic to such a process. Yet without a continual commitment to truth, and without social processes and institutions supportive of truth, a society will more readily devalue free speech and resort to censorship. Like the judicial system, the political system also has become less supportive of truth-finding.

TRUTH AND THE POLITICAL PROCESS

The political system presents the only institution or opportunity for the public to democratically agree upon and implement social truth. Consequently, this institution was intended as a primary beneficiary of the First Amendment and free speech. As envisioned by the founders, America's political system would produce through the open marketplace of free speech the political truth upon which the viability of self-government so depended. According to this theory, a democratic politics based on free speech would produce a more objective and rational social truth than would the old aristocratic and monarchical systems of government prevailing in Europe. This pragmatic view of truth relied on the willingness of political combatants to set aside their differences in the face of such objective truth.

Contrary to the hopes and expectations of the founders, however, American politics has drifted a long way from the pragmatic model. As with the judicial system, it has become more permanently adversarial. It has also become more ideologically divisive, and the ideological differences are becoming more deeply engrained.

The chief political disputes of the last several years have been intensely ideological in nature, with no clear resolution and with no clear relevance to social problems. The 1988 presidential campaign demonstrated this type of ideological politics. The main issues centered on flag-burning, recitation of the Pledge of Allegiance, abortion, and capital punishment. Even if we passed laws to outlaw desecration of the flag, to mandate recitation of the Pledge of Allegiance in schools, and to allow capital punishment, we would be no closer to resolution of the real underlying problems: social unity and crime control. And the moral issue of abortion might never be solved by legislation or constitutional law. Yet, rather than discuss the solutions to social problems like education, poverty, crime, and the environment, our political system seems increasingly prone to focus on purely ideological issues that have no objective resolution. Indeed, it was this type of politics that American pragmatism sought to avoid.

Perhaps politics has become more ideological because the political problems and issues have become so complex. So much information exists on the problem of poverty and social welfare policy, for instance, that the vast majority of voters cannot comprehend it all. In the face of such overwhelming complexity, the public perhaps resorts to a simple but clear ideological orientation toward the problem. Some adopt the ideology that America is a land of individual independence and that public aid to the poor will only breed corruption and dependence. Others believe that society should always aid those of its more unfortunate members and that public aid is a moral obligation of a good society, regardless of what effects welfare dependence might breed or how much it might cost. Thus, issues are decided on ideology instead of on facts. This ideological orientation, however, often prevents the attainment of any social truth and precludes agreement on any objective solution to the problem.

Ideological orientations have become so engrained that they present a nearly insurmountable barrier to objective agreement or social truth. Conservatives frequently refuse to believe that social welfare programs might actually lift persons out of poverty and into a productive life, and liberals often deny evidence of corruption in such programs or that those programs might actually hurt some recipients. When Daniel Patrick Moynihan, as an advisor to Lyndon Johnson in 1965, talked about the "tangle of pathology" that resulted from the breakdown of ghetto family life, many liberals denounced him as a racist. Yet today we are learning that indeed the breakdown of family life does exert a negative effect on those involved. Thus, the ideological orientation of modern politics inhibits the nurturing of political truth.

The more ideological our notion of truth becomes, the less searching we do for objective truth and the less value we place on free speech and debate. In this fast-paced and complex world, ideological orientations provide an easy stepping stone over the truth. Rather than undergoing the long and arduous process of truth-searching through robust debate of a vast array of complex facts, individuals can simply apply their ideological views and reach a much quicker and more resolute conclusion on a political issue.

There is also an increasing scarcity of processes and institutions geared to support the public's search for social truth through reasoned judgments or opinions on social issues. While only through an open exchange of viewpoints can a society hope to reach some agreement on a matter of social truth, few opportunities for such debate seem to exist. Political parties have become increasingly isolated from the general public and also seem to have no interest in doing anything but sponsoring candidates for elections, and the media has become so concentrated and specialized that few individuals can actually participate in any social communication through that forum. Consequently, not many opportunities exist for the type of social debate needed to arrive at political truth.

Therefore, a very weak truth-building stage is incorporated into the political process. In contemporary politics there are only victories and losses – rarely is a sense of truth achieved. As demonstrated by the predominance of political consultants and fundraisers in the political arena, we as a democratic society are learning how to wage political battle more than we are learning how to reach the truth through a common process of agreement.

The ideological and combative orientation of contemporary politics not only deviates from the pragmatic orientation, but can even directly oppose the search for objective truth. Several examples illustrate this point. Recently, the secretary of Health and Human Services blocked a proposed study of teenage sexual behavior that had been approved by the Public Health Service.[10] Secretary Louis Sullivan reacted to complaints from conservatives that the survey contained too many explicit questions. According to one such complaining conservative, "We already know teenagers have sex too early, too often and with too many people."[11] Indeed, William Dannemeyer, a Republican congressman, has been successful for two years in blocking an adult sex survey proposed by the National Institute of Health.

This ideological rejection of the discovery or even discussion of factual information has also occurred with the highly emotional topics of AIDS and abortion. In his memoirs, for instance, former Surgeon General C. Everett Koop states that for the first five and a half years of the Reagan administration he was forbidden to even discuss AIDS.[12] Dr. Koop also writes that the administration commanded him to write a report outlining an opposition to abortion on the grounds that it had a negative mental and physical effect on the woman. Though he gathered whatever data supported this argument and ultimately wrote the report, he later admitted that he suspected that the scientific evidence did not support the report's position. Similarly, the Reagan administration enacted federal regulations that prohibited family planning clinics that received any federal funds from even discussing abortion with their patients.[13]

As another example of ideology denying fact, the 1990 census findings revealed how political our treatment of the truth has become. The postcensus investigation indicated that the census had missed approximately 5.3 million people. Though the aim of the census is to gather a truthful picture of American society and to use this picture to create social policy, a dispute quickly emerged as to whether the official census would be adjusted to account for the original error. However, because the new figures could give additional political power to certain areas and because they might indicate the existence of more severe social problems, the government refused to recognize them.

In addition to the ideological orientation of politics, another development that has affected the search for social truth has been the rise of interest-group politics. This brand of politics has affected the role of political truth insofar as political decisions are not made on the basis of judgments of truth or fact, but on the basis of which particular interest group possesses the most power. The political process consequently aims at satisfying the demands of organized groups rather than searching for social truth on which to base political decisions. Like ideological politics, interest-group politics offers an easy alternative to the more grueling task of basing political actions on a determination of social truth.

The guiding principle behind interest-group politics has been the pure power of the group – a principle that in effect has replaced democratically determined social truth as the standard for political action. Thus, the connection between political decisions and social truth is weakened. Furthermore, interest groups have often sought to avoid the democratic process by establishing a system of rights and entitlements that would guarantee fulfillment of their interests regardless of popular opinion. This bypassing of the democratic process has removed any need to attain social truth through the political system.

Under interest-group politics, debate about the truth of particular social problems and their remedies becomes irrelevant and unnecessary. Instead, such decisions and judgments are left, not to the market-place of debate, but to the marketplace of interest-group power. Because the chosen path to political governance is paved by the loyalty and power of interest groups, politicians lack the will or courage to speak frankly about the issues facing these groups when the logical remedies may not coincide with the agendas of the particular group. For instance, if the union leadership decides that protectionism favors the working person, politicians take up that cause even in the face of evidence to the contrary.

One final, although certainly not minor, political obstacle to truth lies in the increasing institutionalization of secrecy and deceit. A democracy relies upon open debate and a full disclosure of all facts relevant to public issues. The workings of Congress reflect this recognition. Robust debate and full inquiries into all contemplated legislation characterize the function and role of a democratic government. Yet since the end of World War II, as the nation and government have become more focused on foreign policy, an increasing element of secrecy has crept into the functioning and policy-making of government.

The nation's foreign policy, which held unprecedented importance during the Cold War era, and its working agents such as the CIA, are wrapped in a cloud of secrecy, removed from the open debate that characterizes domestic issues. Consequently, the level of secrecy attached to the workings of government – a government continually absorbed in foreign policy – has also risen. And as secrecy becomes more prevalent, the public becomes more accustomed to censorship as a necessary protection of society. This increased role of secrecy, however, contradicts the essential nature of democratic government. It also gradually lulls the populace into accepting a lower level of debate and openness in the general political life of the nation and into ignoring both the duty and the right to demand that politics be devoted to the discovery and implementation of social truth.

There is a strange irony in the build-up of government agencies of secrecy like the CIA, based on the justification that such agencies are vitally necessary for national survival. While the constitutional framers saw truth and open debate as necessary for the protection and maintenance of democratic government, Americans in the latter twentieth century have come to accept that undemocratic institutions of secrecy are in fact necessary to protect their democratic nation. Perhaps the increased perception of foreign threats simply underlay that development, but nonetheless the effect has been to downgrade the pursuit of social truth in the process of self-government.

In *Freedom at Risk: Secrecy, Censorship and Repression in the 1980s*, Richard O. Curry describes the Reagan administration's obsession with secrecy and its increasing classification of government documents and information. According to Curry, the administration institutionalized secrecy and censorship in ways that will be difficult or impossible to eradicate in the future. This institutionalization of secrecy is reflected by a recent request by a group of historians to lift what it claimed was excessive government secrecy toward United States foreign policy. According to the Organization of American Historians, the integrity of the series entitled *Foreign Relations of the United States* has been undermined by the alarming number of incomplete and absent documents.

Unfortunately, the cloaking and manipulation of the truth in American public life is not confined to the foreign policy arena. Even the public dialogue of our highest political officials has drifted far from the kind of truthful public discourse needed in a democracy. Indeed, political language in the era of the media sound-bite has become more a language of manipulation than of honesty and truth. Consequently, the public no longer sufficiently expects and demands that its politicians be open and truthful.

Doubletalk and ceremonial lies abound in the language of political officials. Every four years we hear from all the potential candidates that they are not actively seeking the presidency. Of course, every political victory is claimed by every politician, and every defeat or failure is denied by all. Like most presidential candidates before him, George Bush told the American public in 1988 that he had picked Dan Quayle as the running mate best qualified to assume the presidency in the event of the president's death. Americans all knew that the statement was not true, but their frustration was directed at Mr. Quayle for being chosen, not at Mr. Bush for telling a political untruth. Likewise, when President Bush said he nominated Clarence Thomas without regard to his race or ideology and as simply the best man on the merits for the Supreme Court, most of the public knew that statement to be the untruth that it was. Indeed, contrast the president's failure to state the obvious with Lyndon Johnson's frank explanation of his reasons for nominating Thurgood Marshall in 1967: "I believe it is the right thing to do, the right time to do it, the right man and the right place."

As a result of this political dialogue that jockeys with the truth, the public has come to discount or even ignore the speech of its political officials. Unfortunately, in so doing, the public's expectation of truth through the political process is also diminished.

The rise of media politics and the reliance on advertising agencies for campaign rhetoric has also contributed to a political dialogue that seems largely indifferent to the truth. Indeed, truth has simply become one of many options to choose among in speaking to the public. Image unfortunately has often eclipsed truth in political dialogue.

Of course, the political doubletalk and media sound-bites have nowhere near the negative effect on truth as do outright deception and lies by public officials. Regrettably, instances of the latter type have been all too common in recent years. Beginning with Watergate, the secret bombing of Cambodia, the unexplained pardon of Richard Nixon, the covert dealings of the CIA, and extending through the Iran-Contra debacle, Abscam, the military fraud scandals of the 1980s, and the unprecedented number of ethical and conflict of interest violations by members of the Reagan administration, Americans have been almost continually exposed to deceit and falsehoods perpetrated by their public officials. A more recent example has occurred in the hearings on the nomination of Robert Gates as head of the CIA. His denial of knowledge of the Iran-Contra affair is directly contradicted by the testimony of colleagues who swore they informed him of the illegal scheme at least six times. Most regrettably, Mr. Gates's apparent lack of honesty has raised no strong public outcry, nor has it been met with any apparent reaction by the president, who seems unconcerned with either the discovery or revelation of truth.

There is little wonder that the public today not only does not expect truth to result from the political process, it does not even trust its government or its officials to refrain from intentional deceit. The majority of Americans now "believe that the level of honesty among professionals, business people and government officials has dropped alarmingly in the past few decades."[14] Although democracy demands that its leaders tell the truth and provide all the facts, contemporary politicians seem more concerned with how to hide facts—for example, the facts of the savings and loan problem, the casualties of the Gulf War, the impact on the budget deficit of spending programs and tax cuts—and the public seems content not knowing all of the unpleasant facts. This relegation of truth to second-class status, however, carries important consequences for America's attitude toward censorship. If truth becomes less important, free speech becomes less valued. And hence it is little wonder that, when dealing with censorship issues during the 1980s, the public was less willing to accept the argument that free speech was necessary for the attainment of truth.

TRUTH AND THE UNIVERSITY

The pursuit of truth in the judicial and political arenas has become muddled, subordinated, and even sometimes discarded. To the cynic, of course, the expectation that anything resembling truth will come from lawyers or politicians is foolhardy and ludicrous. Teachers, however, are quite another matter. The school and the classroom are supposed to be enclaves of truth. Unfortunately, education has been subjected to the same kind of ideological battles that have characterized the political system. Truth has consequently become less of an objective, pragmatic pursuit and more of an ideological orientation.

The battle over textbooks in the nation's public school systems reflects this growing ideological orientation. Religious fundamentalists oppose the teaching of evolution and secular humanism. They advocate, instead, the use of books that stress traditional family values, Christian morality, patriotism, and the theory of creationism. At the other end of the ideological spectrum, gay and lesbian groups complain that history textbooks do not recognize the contributions to society made by gays and lesbians. African-Americans object to the use of the novel *The Adventures of Huckleberry Finn* because of its derogatory depictions of blacks. Feminists oppose books that contain sexist references or cast women in stereotyped roles. Some conservatives, on the other hand, disagree with textbook discussions on such supposedly un-American subjects as feminism, unions, socialism, and secular humanism.

These textbook battles are conducted primarily with a focus on ideology, not with an objective view of the pursuit of truth. Indeed, the censorship attempts that frequently result from these ideological battles try to use the force of law to implant ideology in the classroom and to stunt the pursuit of objective truth through robust debate.

Although these battles continue to rage in the nation's primary and secondary schools, perhaps the most dramatic attempts at censorship are occurring in higher education. Ideological and political battles in America's colleges and universities are exerting a significant chill on the exercise of free speech at those institutions.

Of all the social institutions traditionally concerned with rational truth, the university clearly stands at the top. Indeed, the American respect for education and the belief that progress flows from a pursuit of truth has led to the development in this country of the finest system of higher education in the world. Despite American cynicism toward politics and politicians, the belief in the university is solid and long standing. It is even solid enough to keep students and their parents writing checks for the astronomically high tuition payments. An enduring American belief is in the power of education to provide for a better future.

Dedicated to the pursuit of truth as they are, the universities have traditionally been at the forefront of defending the First Amendment and the value of free expression. Perhaps nowhere else in American life has free speech and unhindered debate existed as it has on college campuses. And this open debate has been seen as vital to the pursuit of truth.

Yet, just as the role of truth has changed in the political arena, so too has it changed in the academic setting. In response to a new awareness of the nation's cultural diversity and to a reaction against traditional views of American society and values, scholarship in the humanities and liberal arts areas has taken on a more relativist view of truth. Hesitant to impose the values or perspectives of traditional Western culture on students of diverse backgrounds, the university is moving away from not only a Western-oriented education but also from a view of any consensus or objective truth altogether.

As in the political arena, the academic community is tending to take a more ideological view of truth. Consequently, and also similar to the political realm, the academic world is treating the truth somewhat like a political battle. Indeed, as truth becomes ideological, it becomes political.

In connection with this ideological orientation, truth is also taking on an interest-group characteristic. Since truth is pluralistic and relative, it cannot be attained without the proper mix of participants in the education process. Thus, the drive for diversity in faculty and student bodies attains importance not only in building a valuable and diverse learning environment, but in constituting the very definition and embodiment of truth as well. Without the proper mix of groups and personnel, any learning is seen as tainted with a badge of unenlightened falsehood.

An ideological view of truth and the corresponding interest-group approach to education has produced an ambiguous attitude toward truth. Consequently, the previously impassioned belief of the academic community in free speech has also weakened. The best example of this change in free speech attitudes has occurred with the politically correct movement.

This movement refers to the well-publicized trend at many universities to judge ideas and speech by their political correctness – that is, on the basis of which groups the speech might offend or whether the speech supports a particular political ideology. Political correctness also refers to the policing of sensitive speech on campuses in an effort to wipe out certain types of expressions, such as racist, sexist, and discriminatory speech. Although the strength and extent of this movement are still not completely known, its existence at some very prominent campuses is unquestioned.

In essence, the politically correct movement reflects an ideological approach to education that diminishes the importance of free speech. Led by activists seeking to combat the racism and sexism they see in American culture, political correctness judges speech and ideas by whether they promote or oppress certain minority or victimized groups in society. Consequently, in the political struggle on campuses, tolerance toward speech deemed politically incorrect has declined. This merging of scholarship with politics indicates a decline in the value of both the pursuit of objective truth and of the freedom of expression. As Annette Kolodny, dean of the humanities faculty at the University of Arizona, admits: "I see my scholarship as an extension of my political activism."[15]

The remarkable aspect of the politically correct movement is that it is being led by individuals who, during the 1960s, bitterly fought for freedom of expression on college campuses. The Berkeley free speech movement, for instance, symbolized a generation seeking greater openness and freedom in society. In the course of the protests over Vietnam and civil rights, students fought college administrators for greater freedom of expression. In the classroom, students in the 1960s likewise sought to expand the curriculum and class discussions to include the controversial ideas and events of the time. Contrary to this history, however, many of today's college faculty and administrators, though they were the dissenters in the 1960s, are trying to silence dissident speech in the 1990s.

Critics have claimed that the politically correct movement attempts to turn the college curriculum into a political indoctrination course and that the enforcers of political correctness are trying to achieve their goals through intimidation rather than persuasion and debate. As such, political correctness has subordinated the pursuit of truth and the free expression of ideas. Indeed, insofar as the politically correct movement seeks to eliminate or exclude certain speech from the campus, it is a censorship crusade.

According to the rules of political correctness, it is considered racist to speak of the rights of the individual when they conflict with the prevailing opinion of the particular racial community, it is taboo to debate the moral fitness of homosexuals as parents, and it is sexist to order a Domino's pizza because the company's chairman donates money to an antiabortion group.[16] On politically correct campuses, distasteful views are labeled unacceptable. Political agendas, rather than logic and rationality, govern the course of education and the rules for speech. According to Leon Botstein, president of New York's Bard College: "Nobody wants to listen to the other side. On many campuses, you really have a culture of forbidden questions."[17]

Dinesh D'Souza, a critic of political correctness on college campuses, argues that students are not receiving a liberal education but are getting the diametrically opposite – an education in closed-mindedness and intolerance.[18] As D'Souza argues, truth is the basis for freedom, and truth and education rest in the free expression of ideas. Yet he finds in higher education a rising tide of thought control and intellectual dishonesty that is subverting the true purpose of education and freedom of speech. To avoid offending the politically correct watchdogs, according to D'Souza, professors must carefully censor the material they present in the classroom.

In a politically correct educational environment, the search for truth through free speech is subverted by the claim that what is true is what is ideologically acceptable. This ideologically doctrinaire approach to education and to truth obviously undermines the cornerstone of education—free and open debate. The politically correct movement, which tries to attain truth through rules about what can and cannot be discussed, ultimately contradicts the American tradition of education that truth can only be acquired through open discussion.

An examination of several publicized instances of political correctness demonstrates the censoring effect of this movement:

- City College of New York punished a professor for writing that "on average, blacks are significantly less intelligent than whites." At the same time, it took no action against another professor who argued that abundant skin pigment in blacks gives them intellectual and physical advantages over whites.[19]

- An emeritus professor at the University of Missouri, who criticized an opinion by Supreme Court Justice Thurgood Marshall, received complaints from a black student and was sent to the dean of minority affairs.

- At the University of Michigan, a young man expressed the opinion that homosexuality is immoral. He was sent to a harassment officer who ordered the student to complete six weeks of sensitivity training; later he was directed to write an essay of self-recrimination under the title "I Was Wrong," which later was published in the school newspaper.

- The student newspaper at Vassar College lost its funding after editors called a black undergraduate a hypocrite for making anti-Semitic remarks while at the same time publicly condemning bigotry.

- Al Gini, a professor at Loyola University in Chicago who had won three teacher-of-the-year awards, was branded a racist and subjected to an eight-month investigation after he told his class that the term "nigger" was no longer socially acceptable.

- A Harvard professor, Stephen Thernstrom, was sanctioned after having used the terms "Indians," instead of "Native Americans," and "Oriental," with its imperialistic overtones, in class. In addition, he had assigned a book that included an argument against affirmative action. Not only was this found to be a racist opinion, but professor Thernstrom's endorsement of Patrick Moynihan's belief that the breakup of the black family was a cause of persistent black poverty was also considered a racist idea.

- Another Harvard professor, Bernard Bailyn, a winner of two Pulitzer Prizes, was attacked for reading in class from the diary of a Southern planter without giving equal time to the recollections of a slave. According to students, this amounted to a defense of slavery. Bailyn argued, however, that such equal time was impossible because no journals, diaries, or letters written by slaves had ever been found.

- At Santa Monica College, the social science department censured an economics professor who argued that ethnic and gender-based studies "sidetrack students who could otherwise gain useful disciplines or skills."[20]

- Christina Hoff Sommers, a professor of philosophy at Clark University, refused to sign a course-proposal form that would have required her to explain how she had incorporated pluralistic views into her teaching.

- Several schools have punished students for expressing religious objections to homosexuality, and at the University of Washington, for questioning a professor's assertion that lesbians make the best mothers.[21]

- A Michigan professor stopped teaching a particular class rather than face charges of racial insensitivity when he had students read the portions of Malcolm X's autobiography in which Malcolm describes himself as a pimp and a thief.

- Alan Gribben, a professor of English at the University of Texas, was denounced as a racist when he voted against a master's level program in Third World and minority literature and again when he protested the designation as required reading of material with a pronounced left-wing slant.

- At the University of Pennsylvania, a student on a committee for diversity education expressed in a memo her "deep regard for the individual and . . . desire to protect the freedoms of all members of society." A university administrator circled this passage and commented that "this is a red flag phrase today, which is considered by many to be racist. Arguments that champion the individual over the group ultimately privileges [sic] the individuals belonging to the largest or dominant group."[22]

- Tufts University declared that the speech of its students and faculty be regulated according to zone. For instance, in public areas, speech is unregulated; in classrooms and dining halls, derogatory speech is prohibited; and in dormitories, offensive remarks that violate a student's right to privacy are subject to punishment.

As can be seen, the politically correct weapon stigmatizes dissenting speech as misguided, wrong, and a threat to society. The obvious chilling of free speech seems an acceptable price to pay for an ideological and political victory. A leader of the student government at Stanford University summarized this attitude: "What we are proposing is not completely in line with the First Amendment. But I'm not sure it should be."[23] And Kate Fahey, an associate dean at Mount Holyoke College, suggested that freedoms of speech depend on the answers to several questions: "[W]hat is it going to do to our community? Is it going to damage us?"[24]

As disturbing as this cavalier attitude toward free speech is, it is even more troubling when seen in the nation's law schools. In those schools the reverence for free speech and the First Amendment should preclude any ideological interference with truth. Unfortunately, the politically correct movement is taking its toll on free speech in the law school just as it is in the university at large. A few examples will demonstrate this assault on speech:

- At Harvard Law School, visiting professor Ian Macneil found himself the target of organized vilification in 1989 by the Harvard Women's Law Association. The group accused Macneil of sexism because by quoting from Byron's poem "Don Juan" he encouraged domination of women and even sexual harassment. He also "encouraged sexist thought" by using such terms as "grandfather clause" and "strawman."[25] The Harvard administration reportedly gave no support to Macneil in defending the charges.
- Students at New York University School of Law organized a protest against a required hypothetical case that focused on a lesbian mother fighting for custody of her child.
- A student at Berkeley School of Law was repeatedly booed and hissed for arguing a conservative position.[26]

This intolerance of ideas that contradict certain philosophical or political tenets has been increasingly accompanied by bans on speech. Dozens of universities have introduced tough new codes prohibiting speech that leads to, among other things, a "demeaning atmosphere."[27] More than one hundred schools have adopted harassment codes that punish students who utter prejudiced comments.[28] The University of Michigan, for instance, enacted a code that punishes any speech that stigmatizes or victimizes an individual on the basis of any one of twelve criteria. And the University of Connecticut issued a proclamation banning "inappropriately directed laughter" and "conspicuous exclusion of students from conversations."

These kinds of speech codes, however, are often counterproductive. By suppressing all forms of discriminatory or offensive speech, such codes merely drive prejudices underground where they can only worsen. Indeed, racial prejudice can only be eliminated by letting people truly confront those prejudices through openly expressing them and subjecting them to the counterspeech of others. Perhaps for these reasons the proliferation of speech codes at American universities has caused great alarm.

In response to these occurrences of campus intolerance, a significant number of academicians have voiced a concern for free expression. Donald Kagan, a dean at Yale University, remarked that in many universities, "there is an imposed conformity of opinion. It takes real courage to oppose the orthodoxies. To tell you the truth, I was a student during the days of Joseph McCarthy, and there is less freedom now than there was then."[29] Moreover, an association of university faculty, the National Association of Scholars (NAS), has been formed to combat political correctness. The NAS has approximately 1,400 members and twenty-five chapters nationwide.

The formation of NAS chapters, however, has brought harsh reactions from some politically correct advocates. For instance, when Duke University scholar James David Barber, author of *The Presidential Character* and past president of Amnesty International, tried to establish an NAS chapter at Duke, he was sharply attacked by Professor Stanley Fish, chairman of Duke's English department and a staunch advocate of political correctness. In response to the imminent formation of an NAS chapter, professor Fish wrote to the provost that any faculty members belonging to the NAS should not be appointed to key committees involving tenure or curriculum decisions – an obvious attempted denial of speech and association freedoms of certain faculty opposing the politically correct movement.

Faculty and administrators who have been criticized for promoting political correctness do not deny that in attempting to combat racism some students have become overly sensitive and that some college speech codes may have infringed on constitutional rights. They even concede that inflammatory incidents of censorship and intellectual bullying did take place at some institutions, including the University of California at Berkeley. There, students invaded a lecture hall and shouted down a professor who had written that affirmative action admissions were harming the academic quality of the university. And Hispanic students at Arizona State University demanded that an appearance by Linda Chavez, the former director of the U.S. Commission on Civil Rights and a critic of bilingual education, be canceled.[30]

If the politically correct movement is any indication of future trends, education is increasingly becoming a political endeavor and a crusade for political indoctrination.

Another example of the political treatment of truth and knowledge within the university lies in the conflict over the teaching of history. Like political correctness, the interpretation of history is shifting from an exercise in scholarship to one in politics. Indeed, the study of the history of Western civilization is becoming increasingly politically incorrect. Those academics who oppose the traditional teaching of Western civilization argue that the United States is undergoing a multicultural revolution in which differences should be highlighted and studied without the prism of a Western viewpoint. They claim that Western philosophy and civilization reflect the "great white man theory of history" – a history inapplicable and oppressive to a multicultural

United States.[31] Thus, the problem with the traditional curriculum is that it "teaches all of us to see the world through the eyes of privileged, white, European males and to adopt their interests and perspectives as our own."[32]

Seeking to replace the Western view of history are various ethnic-focused interpretations. For instance, to satisfy the demands of various political and community activists, New York State officials have responded to pressure from Native American leaders by revamping the state high school curriculum to include the historically questionable assertion that the U.S. Constitution was based on the political system of the Iroquois Confederacy. And in Berkeley, Chicano activist Martha Acevedo blocked adoption of new state-approved textbooks. Citing the depiction of a nineteenth century Hispanic Robin Hood–style figure who is shown in one text on a wanted poster, Acevedo argued that the books lacked positive role models.[33] Thus, history is seemingly becoming more concerned with image, and various ethnic and racial groups are increasingly advocating a history that casts them in a positive light.

Afrocentric history, for example, aims to trace the roots of all civilization – all cultural, philosophical, and scientific development – back to Africa. European culture is presented as nothing more than a bastardized version of African culture, and Asian culture is virtually ignored. Thus, Afrocentricity seeks not just the legitimate goal of enlightening the world to the accomplishments of Africans and African-Americans, but it also seeks to redress the wrongs of European civilization. In essence, this version of history strives primarily to elevate the self-esteem of African-American students. Consequently, not only does human history become controlled by a single operative factor, namely race, but education becomes a tool for ego-nourishment.

Critics of the balkanized or ideological approach to history reflected in Afrocentricity claim that some of the information and theories are erroneous and that some of the proposed curriculum additions are not as significant to the development of human civilization as the weight being afforded them by Afrocentrists.[34] For instance, some Afrocentrists hold that Africans were in the New World even before Columbus's journey and that ancient Greece stole its culture from Africa. Other critics argue that Afrocentrism, like the politically correct movement, is more like an ideology than an academic discipline. They believe that Afrocentrism is an attempt to improve black students' self-esteem rather than to correct the historical record. Indeed, if Eurocentric history is an inaccurate depiction of history and a creation by white males to justify their historic pattern of power and oppression, a replacement of Eurocentrism with Afrocentrism may simply be trading one orthodoxy for another.

While the boosting of African-American students' self-confidence is a legitimate and worthy social goal, it must not be used to manipulate the truth. Clearly, many of the goals of politically sensitive educators are admirable and highly relevant in the political arena. The purpose of education, however, is to present as broad a spectrum of knowledge as possible, so that truth may result from knowledge. For this purpose, free speech and debate are vital. Yet to the extent that the Afrocentric or politically correct movement ends up restricting the amount of speech on campus or chilling robust debate, it narrows rather than expands the horizons of education.

To criticize the impact of political correctness on free speech is not to say that education should not change so as to incorporate a recognition of America's multiculturalism. Indeed, as American society and values change, the academic community must also deal with deep and perplexing questions about its intellectual and institutional life. It must wrestle with how to incorporate the pluralistic nature of society into American education. It must examine how education can best guide society through its cultural problems and its previous injustices to minorities. And it must grapple with determining the theories of human nature and relationships that will prevail in a multicultural society. All of these are worthy goals, but the treatment of truth and free speech must be examined in the way these goals are pursued. By many accounts, it appears that a number of universities and educators are adopting a political or ideological view of truth in their quest to reform education. In doing so, however, they have sacrificed the values of free speech and have opened the door to censorship.

This politicization of education will undoubtedly affect society's value of free speech and its willingness to resort to censorship of undesirable or irritating speech. Furthermore, the current censorship existing on at least some college campuses demonstrates that it is not just conservative reactionaries who resort to censorship—so also do leftists and liberals. Indeed, the judgment by some scholars is that "the conditions of free speech and open debate have evaporated on the campus and have been replaced by timidity and intimidation."[35]

Instead of a place of objective scholarly pursuit of truth, the university may be becoming the site, just as is politics, of interest-group struggles over ideology and power. And contrary to the interest of truth, the university may be becoming more ideological and less rational and tolerant, and may be encouraging a less civil form of discourse. Unfortunately, the incivility that seems to be characterizing academic dialogue indicates a less than treasured value of the pursuit of truth. Indeed, the pursuit of truth should not have to be the kind of ideological, uncivil war that seems to be taking place in academe.

CONCLUSION

Truth is what we so desire in life. The power of the confessional lies in the rare opportunity to express the truth. How often we read a story or an account and anxiously await the end so that the truth be known. Indeed, Americans, like anyone else, want to know the truth. The most popular movies and television programs are, after all, those based on a true story.

Therefore, one hardly ever hears that censorship in America may result at least partly because of America's attitude toward the truth. And though the desire for truth may never diminish, perhaps the nature of truth we expect or demand changes. Such a change, as this discussion has argued, in turn poses consequences for our attitudes toward freedom of expression and censorship.

Truth in America has become more of a battle than a discovery. It has become more a result of power than of rationality and persuasion. It has become more an ideology and political result than an objective wisdom that can be agreed upon. And it has become less dependent on speech and debate. Truth as a product of ideas competing with each other in the marketplace of debate seems to be a somewhat outmoded idea. Perhaps this is partly why we have not resolved our preoccupation and continual reversion to censorship.

Yet if anything, this discussion of truth has debunked the notion that only freedom-haters and reactionary conservatives engage in censorship. Indeed, the censorship of the politically correct movement is inspired by liberals who fought for free speech rights in the 1960s and 1970s. Though dedicated certainly, at one time, to freedom of expression, these liberals have perhaps come to tolerate some forms of censorship because of a new identity they want to create for a multicultural America.

The Search for
American Identity

America has been, and still is, a nation in search of definition. Perhaps that is why speech has been so prominent. Speech has become America's only defining mark. It has become the public face of America. With the progression of time, speech has increasingly become the defining element of national identity. Particularly in this advanced media age, speech symbolizes what the nation and its people are all about. Indeed, almost all other traditional signs of national identity have disappeared.

As a pluralistic and multicultural society, America has no racial, ethnic, cultural, or religious identity. For most nations of the world, nationality is simply a reaffirmation of a long-standing racial or ethnic commonality. The recent separatist movements in former Yugoslavia and the former Soviet Union, for instance, were crusades to once again harmonize a people's ethnic and national identities. As an immigrant nation, however, America has no inherited national identity. It became a nation that was defined by the first settlers and that has subsequently been defined by each new wave of immigrants and each new generation. Compared with the other countries and societies from which the immigrants came, America developed relatively loose bonds of culture, ethnicity, and religion. With the demographic ingredients in its melting pot changing with each generation, the finished brew has often been difficult to identify.

Race, religion, and ethnic origin form rather specific and enduring marks of national identity. Without those identifying traits, America has undergone periodic social and political struggles for identity. The Jeffersonian and Jacksonian reform movements, for instance, injected a more common person identity into American democracy and revolted against the elitist nature of society. The Civil War period also witnessed a profound struggle for American identity. The outcome was that Southern culture would not be the national culture and that the horrible institution of slavery would cease. The reform movements of populism and progressivism subsequently tried to reinvigorate democratic culture and sought to transform America from a land ruled by Eastern industrial monopolists and return it to the individualistic values of freedom and democracy advocated by Thomas Jefferson. And the New Deal era initiated a process of social inclusion aimed at minorities and outgroups that had previously received little recognition. This process continued with the civil rights and women's movements, and it fostered a new awareness of the unique diversity and pluralism of American society. Indeed, Americans are only now coming to fully realize an identity that has always existed in reality: America is a country of cultural diversity and pluralism. The multicultural movement, particularly in higher education, demonstrates this recognition of American identity.

In a recent *Time* essay addressing the multicultural movement and the cultural conflicts raised by this movement, Robert Hughes discussed the ambiguous sense of national identity underlying such conflicts:

There never was a core America in which everyone looked the same, spoke the same language, worshipped the same gods and believed the same things. America is a construction of mind, not of race or inherited class or ancestral territory. It is a creed born of immigration, of the jostling of scores of tribes that become American to the extent to which they can negotiate accommodations with one another. The fact remains that America is a collective act of the imagination whose making never ends, and once that sense of collectivity and mutual respect is broken, the possibilities of American-ness begin to unravel. America is a place filled with diversity, unsettled histories, images impinging on one another and spawning unexpected shapes.[1]

Like every nation, America needs an identity, particularly given its diverse and pluralistic society. Unlike most other nations, however, America must define itself—it does not have a common origin or national evolution to provide such a definition. The geographic boundaries of nationhood are never enough to confer a sense of social identity. Indeed, the separatist movements around the world in the last several years illustrate the futility of relying on mere geographic boundaries.

Even the American Civil War demonstrates the inability of political or geographic boundaries to produce national identity and solidarity. The cultures and symbols of the Northern and Southern societies were so different that they could not peacefully coexist in one nation. A common identity had to be created, even if it took a war to do so.

In the American experience, the concept of nationhood has been adequate as a socially defining or unifying force only in certain limited circumstances. These circumstances have revolved around international competition, whether it be military or athletic competition. During war, Americans often unify around their nation and its military endeavors. For that purpose, the national identity becomes simply the nation's geopolitical boundaries. During other competitions like the Olympic Games, Americans once again find their identity in their national label. But with just about everything else, Americans need more than mere national boundaries to instill a sense of social identity and to create a feeling of patriotism.

The indications of a national yearning for identity are ever present. The renewed interest in the teaching of values in the schools and the incorporation of certain moral or individual values into the political discussion of social welfare policies demonstrate a desire for some social or cultural identity. Likewise, the public interest in genealogy suggests an underlying need for some kind of social or historical identity. This interest reflects a yearning in our rapidly changing society for a genuine historical identity through long-lost traditions and values. Yet the most common way of forging an identity in contemporary America has been through the adherence to common national symbols and through expression of certain values seen to be inherently American.

In the place of ethnic, cultural, or racial identities, America has assumed symbolic identities expressed through speech. With the breakdown of many traditional forms of community and with the increasing prevalence and power of the mass media, speech often becomes the only common trait or image that can define identity. However, the symbolic identities created by speech do not simply fill a void caused by a lack of other ethnic or cultural markings of national identity; they also result from a conscious effort to create a nation out of a set of visions, ideals, and symbols. When the Puritans settled in the Massachusetts Bay Colony, they identified it according to their vision of a "city on a hill" with a messianic purpose. Indeed, the United States is the only nation born out of a belief in symbols and ideas, as expressed in the Declaration of Independence and perpetuated in the national mythology of America as a land of freedom, independence, and virtue.

Just as the break from England was the first act in the creation of a national identity, the Declaration of Independence was America's first tangible definition of identity. Thus, from the birth of American nationhood, the country has been defined by the words and symbols it expresses.

Besides being defined by symbols, however, America also stands as a symbol to the rest of the world. Thus, symbolism becomes not only our definition of America, but the international image of America. As the advocates for democracy in Russia, Eastern Europe, and China during the last several years have looked for guidance, America has stood as a symbol of freedom and prosperity. It has held a mythical status, full of emotive powers. It has symbolized the future promise of freedom, self-determination, and economic opportunity. Indeed, the international reverence for the symbolism of America revealed itself in the passionate display of American flags and placards among the crowds of democratic protestors in Eastern Europe.

With the world tuned into the American media, such symbolic identity is fairly easy to transmit and perpetuate. Perhaps more than any other nation, America concerns itself as much with its symbolism as with its specific actions. While, for instance, most other countries are defined by their history, demographic makeup or economic endeavors, American identity is defined by symbols rather than any specific or concrete aspect of society. Indeed, the popularity and rhetoric of Ronald Reagan demonstrated that this country is one sustained by a set of national symbols. And speech is the primary expression of that symbolism.

As a result of the American search for identity through speech and symbolism, censorship has often played a role in the social conflict inherent in the process of national self-definition. With the national identity continually a matter of debate and definition, the opportunity exists for each generation to pursue a new identity. And in the battles over social definition, censorship, as does speech, serves as a primary weapon. Since each generation or each social group can attempt to articulate a new national identity, censorship merely becomes the flipside of speech in the struggle for such identity. Therefore, certain kinds of censorship can be linked to the national search for identity through the only common forum or bond in America – speech.

The historical process of American self-definition involves conflicts over at least three basic identifying elements. These include the nation's cultural identity, religious and moral identity, and patriotic identity. In each of these areas of identity, America has experienced and continues to experience censorship campaigns in the attempt to define an identity through speech and expressive symbolism.

The conflict over cultural identity is demonstrated by the multicultural movement on the nation's campuses. Political correctness in higher education reflects the use of censorship in the struggle for cultural definition. Multiculturalism has also come to the media, with minority groups complaining that an unrepresentative press often fails to portray American society as the diverse and culturally pluralistic society it is. In their struggle to redefine America as a multicultural society, these groups often demand censorship of images and speech that portray minorities in a derogatory light.

The recent concern with multiculturalism reflects a long-standing cultural debate in America. That debate centers on the unity of American culture in a land of diverse cultural groups. In addressing this issue, historians have argued over whether American history is one of consensus or conflict. According to consensus historians, there exists a definable American spirit or identity that can be detected throughout history. To them, history has minimized domestic social conflict and has stressed the continuity of the nation's identity and values. Consensus historians believe in the homogeneity of the American experience. Therefore, a particular culture or national character may be defined through history.

Other historians, however, envision a history of conflict. They argue that American history has evolved not through consensus on cultural values, but through conflict between various social and cultural groups. Conflict history denies the existence of a unified national character. Instead, the changing diversity and pluralism of American society have essentially produced a national identity of conflict and turmoil.

This dispute over the meaning of American history and national identity reflects other underlying cultural conflicts that have occurred throughout history. One very pronounced conflict occurred during the 1920s. Following the war and a period of rapid immigration that greatly expanded urban populations, two cultures came in conflict. One represented the older, Puritanical, rural-oriented, and producer-capitalist culture; the other represented the emerging urban, secular, modernist, and consumer-oriented culture. The struggle between these cultures was a conflict of different visions of life. The newer culture was the product of the communications and industrial revolutions of the nineteenth century and was promoted by the new middle class of managers, professionals, and white-collar workers produced by these revolutions. Whereas the older culture called for the development of individual *character* grounded in moral rectitude, the new culture insisted on *personality*. This new culture of consumption was marked by new technologies and institutions (electricity, photography, the department store, and the automobile), new cultural forms (comic books, radio, movies, advertising, and magazines), and new life goals (leisure, recreation, self-fulfillment and celebrity status.)[2]

The confrontation of the two cultures in their struggle to define the national identity produced perhaps the most widespread social censorship campaign yet experienced in American history. The pervasive censorship attempts in literature and motion pictures reflected this cultural struggle. While the newer culture sought expression of its identity in the books it was writing and in the movies it was producing, the older culture sought to retain its identity through censorship of these books and movies. This cultural struggle also spilled over into censorship activities directed against immigrant urban radicals who had protested the war and the capitalist treatment of workers.

In the present age, cultural struggles continue, and censorship continues to reflect these struggles. The politically correct movement, the campaign against bilingualism, and the censorship of black music and African-American nationalist speech reveal the cultural tensions in modern society. In addition to racial and ethnic tensions, struggles over gender relations also characterize the current conflict over cultural identity. This gender conflict was illustrated by the hearings on the nomination of Clarence Thomas to the Supreme Court, in which a former employee, Anita Hill, alleged that Judge Thomas had sexually harassed her. At issue was the language Thomas had used in Hill's presence. Occurring at a time when feminists were advocating a new national language free of sexist speech, the Thomas-Hill dispute exemplified the degree to which tensions between the sexes have translated into a controversy over acceptable speech between men and women. As with the censorship of pornography, obscenity, and sexist speech, the Thomas-Hill dispute demonstrated the conflict inherent in the searching for a gender identity of American culture and the pursuit of a civilized culture of social dialogue between men and women.

The cultural struggles in contemporary America are discussed in James Hunter's book, *Culture Wars: The Struggle to Define America*. Though Americans may be increasingly oblivious to politics and to traditional political issues, according to Mr. Hunter, they are particularly sensitive and attentive to cultural matters. In place of such economic issues as income distribution and free trade, Americans now place primary emphasis on cultural issues such as school prayer, condoms for teenagers, the theory of evolution, federal funding for erotic art, and the Pledge of Allegiance. The intensity of conflict on these issues has placed America in "the midst of a culture war" between modernists and fundamentalists. Since this war is often fought on the battleground of the media, censorship becomes a frequently used weapon. In the midst of a "kind of post-modern cultural confusion," where racism tears at the social fabric and flag-burning desecrates the most visible national symbol, many advocates of censorship believe that "some things are more important than free speech."[3]

The second element of American identity – the religious and moral identity – likewise has had a long history of both conflict and censorship. In the struggle for an American identity, religion has historically played a powerful role. Other than the myth of individualism, religion has been perhaps the strongest single ingredient in the nation's cultural meaning and identity.

The presence and influence of civil religion in America attests to the impact of religion on the national identity. The Declaration of Independence gave birth to a new nation based upon "the laws of . . . nature's God" and the belief that all persons "are endowed by their Creator with certain unalienable rights." Religious influences pervade contemporary public life. Political leaders take oaths on the Bible. The inscription "In God We Trust" appears on the currency. Chaplains open sessions of Congress with a prayer.

While religious influences have impacted such various social reform movements as abolition, child welfare, civil rights and the antinuclear movement, they have also affected the national speech and dialogue. Censorship campaigns against pornography, violence, permissiveness, and demonism, for instance, demonstrate the attempt to bring a religious flavor into the national identity.

The purity in print campaign in the 1920s reflected a search for the religious rejuvenation of society.[4] Indeed, the Clean Books Crusade was a religious reaction to the perceived trend in literature representing "a national obliteration of the moral sense."[5] The religiously motivated censorship advocates sought, during a time of the Roaring Twenties, the Jazz Age, and the flapper, a return to earlier days "when everybody belonged to a church."[6] Religious censorship of speech relating to sex, birth control, and divorce – subjects that were being more openly discussed – was a reaction against a cultural identity that had less respect for spiritual values and allowed less religious control over secular life.

Censorship of movies during the 1930s was also heavily influenced and sponsored by religious interests. The Catholic church, which had previously been involved in book censorship through its *Index of Forbidden Books,* became involved in movie censorship with its Legion of Decency. Included in the subjects to be censored, as advocated by the Legion of Decency and adopted by the Motion Picture Producers and Distributors Association (MPPDA), were profanity, nudity, sex hygiene, ridicule of clergy, prostitution, glorification of crime, and men and women in bed together. A special concern of the Legion of Decency were movies that conveyed a sense of guiltlessness and a flaunting of social rules and taboos. Consequently, the movie *Gone with the Wind* faced heavy censorship pressures for its bold use of the word "damn" in the final scene.

After World War II, and in response to the growing power of the television and motion picture industries, religious-sponsored censorship continued. In a society that was rapidly changing in the aftermath of the war and relishing the new freedoms and prosperity of the postwar era, the religious identity of America again became uncertain. Movies like *The Miracle, Baby Doll,* and *Life of Brian,* which dealt with religion in a nontraditional manner, faced censorship pressures from religious groups. Indeed, one of the principles of movie censors was that neither blasphemy nor ridicule of religion would be allowed.[7]

The religious censorship of the 1950s, however, was only a precursor to that of the 1960s and 1970s. With the sexual revolution and the rebellion against traditional values and religious institutions, the historic religious identity of America came under attack. In response, religious groups advocated censorship of magazines like *Playboy,* rock music that advocated sex and glorified demonism, and television programming that flaunted traditional values and sexual taboos. It was during this period that the family hour standards were adopted for television programming during the evening prime time hours. And a new age-classification system, advocated by groups fearing the effect of movies on impressionable youth, was implemented for motion pictures and contained the ratings of G, GP (later PG), R, and X.

The 1980s and 1990s likewise have witnessed a continuation of the religious struggle for America's identity. The rise of religious fundamentalism and the Moral Majority brought a significant increase in censorship pressures. Book censorship in the schools expanded, with attempts to ban the teaching of evolution and secular humanism. Religious groups continued their opposition to movies that appeared disrespectful of religion, as illustrated by the reaction against *The Last Temptation of Christ.* And rock and roll record album covers, reflecting the "un-Christian nature and lifestyles of rock performers and music,"[8] have been regularly burned in religious burning rituals.

Religious censorship also branched out into some new areas of speech, such as the censorship campaign against the NEA and against books that promoted feminism, gay rights, and abortion. Indeed, the increasing politicization of art and culture during the last decade derived in large part from the attempt by religious groups to stop the trend toward a perceived secularization of the national identity.

The almost constant battle over moral and cultural speech issues during the 1980s fundamentally involved a battle over the moral and cultural identity of America. Moreover, throughout history, censorship has often reflected a desire to maintain some religious component of American identity. Consequently, censorship in the religious area has often been a sign of larger cultural struggles. The Scopes trial in 1925, for instance, reflected the identity crisis of a nation torn between traditional religious moral values and modern secular values. The trial was not just a contest over whether evolutionism could be taught in the school. It was an example of the battle for American identity, between

the modernists and fundamentalists and between the religious traditionalists and the secular rationalists. In fact, the debate still rages on
today, despite the 1987 Supreme Court ruling that struck down a Louisiana law requiring the teaching of creationism.[9]

The third, and perhaps most powerful, element of national identity
includes the speech of patriotism or Americanism. Indeed, the struggle
to define America by defining patriotism and Americanism has produced some of the most dramatic examples of twentieth-century censorship.

In their search for national identity, Americans sometimes seek ways
to identify, as Lyndon Johnson so often mentioned, their "fellow Americans." This searching relates to the attempt to define or discover American traits or characteristics, or a sense of Americanness. In a
pluralistic society, such an attempt often proves fruitless. Thus, speech
becomes, by default, the only possible Americanizing trait. Consequently, the censorship of supposedly un-American speech has become
a way to define at least what is *not* part of the American identity.

The use of a concept of Americanism to define the national identity
stems from the belief that the country has been privileged with a
unique mission. From the time the Puritans settled in Massachusetts
Bay Colony, there has been an American belief in a special purpose or
role for the New World. This concept of American exceptionalism contributed to the ideological case for independence from England. It also
inspired a special belief in the progressive powers of American freedom,
democracy, and economic enterprise. And it is what gave so much appeal to the rhetoric of Ronald Reagan, just as it had to that of John
Kennedy. The only problem, of course, is articulating a vision on which
all Americans can agree. In an attempt to define this national vision or
cultural identity, censorship of un-American ideas has often been es-
poused.

The crusade against un-American speech first appeared during the
surge of nationalism following America's entry into World War I.
Though it had become a leading international power, the nagging question facing America involved its national identity. In a country experiencing massive immigration and great social change, and possessing a
national history of only a century and a half, Americans inherited no
obvious answer to that question. Attempting to define and maintain a
national identity, groups like the American Legion began a crusade
against radicalism, un-Americanism, and the foreign influences of immigrants. This crusade involved a forceful attack on the speech rights
of political dissidents such as socialists, Communists and pacifists.
The goal was 100 percent Americanism. And to groups like the American Legion, criticism of the political, economic, or moral values of the
nation was un-American. Other groups wanted the Catholic Chris-

topher Columbus deemphasized in school textbooks, while the Knights of Columbus wanted him placed on a level of admiration equal to George Washington.

In the 1920s, just as later in the 1950s and 1960s, much censorship activity focused on speech involving the espousal of un-American ideas. National sedition laws were passed prohibiting such speech. Suspected radicals were harassed and punished. Books advocating un-American ideas were banned. The Oregon legislature passed a law requiring that schools use no book "which speaks slightingly of the founders of the Republic, or the men who preserved the Union."[10]

Later in the 1950s, the wave of McCarthyism reflected only more intensely the 1920s crusade against un-Americanism. As before, books were closely scrutinized for any criticism of the free enterprise system. The Sons of the American Revolution saw Communist influence in many textbooks and warned of interstate traffic in propaganda books. The Guardians of American Education claimed that schools and colleges were spawning Marxists. Alabama passed a law in 1953 that required publishers to state whether any authors referenced in a book had ever held leftist beliefs. The Daughters of the American Revolution objected to books that described the United States as a democracy rather than a republic.[11] Lists of purportedly subversive books were circulated by various patriotic organizations. In 1961, the Texas House of Representatives passed a resolution stating that history textbooks should emphasize "our glowing and throbbing history of hearts and souls inspired by wonderful American principles and traditions." A group called Texans for America opposed any books that favorably mentioned such un-American ideas as the income tax, social security, unemployment payments, unions, and racial integration. As the group's president said, textbooks should only teach "the American side."[12]

The movie industry was also investigated during the 1950s for any radical or un-American influences. Movies that appeared to be subversive or that favorably depicted Communism or socialism faced immediate censorship pressures. The advocates of this censorship campaign claimed that they were combatting a Communist attempt to set up a base in the United States. However, since the advocates of Communism or socialism were so few in number and so weakly organized, the real underlying motivation to this censorship campaign was an attempt to control the symbolic identity of the nation. Thus, censorship became part of the effort to define America and the essence of Americanism.

Through rejecting un-American speech, censorship expressed the search for the common bond that unites and characterizes America as a society. The notion of Americanism has often been used to denote a particular mix of cultural, racial, religious, and sexual values. Yet perhaps the most visible censorship of un-American speech has occurred in connection with unpatriotic speech. However, like other marks of American identity, patriotism is itself difficult to define. Therefore, in the course of struggling to define the nation through an ambiguous concept of patriotism, censorship often occurs in an attempt to eradicate what some groups feel is unpatriotic, and hence un-American, speech. But it is precisely because patriotism is not clearly defined that censorship attempts are made in an effort to at least negatively define it.

The notion of patriotism constitutes a powerful force in America. Unquestionably, every nation requires the loyalty of its citizens, for without loyalty, laws would not be obeyed, taxes would not be paid, and any national solidarity would erode. Loyalty is also necessary for the goals and endeavors of the nation. The work of the country, whether it be in fighting poverty or developing industry, needs the backing of its citizens. And in the United States, citizen loyalty is often equated with patriotism.

Like national identity, patriotism must be defined. It must take some coherent shape. With some nations, patriotism seems to arise naturally and easily. In Ireland, for instance, a show of patriotism occurs every night when the bars and discos close down. After a night of revelry, the national anthem is played and all patrons stand and sing along. It is a sight nonexistent in the United States.

Throughout its history, America has struggled with reaching a consensus on patriotism. Because the national identity is not often clearly defined, however, any sense of patriotism becomes equally vague and uncertain. And like the other forms of national identity, Americans have struggled with defining patriotism through speech and symbols.

Not surprisingly, patriotic spirit has been strongest when the nation has faced monumental crises or threats. During the world wars, the country displayed a passionate sense of patriotism, as it did during much of the New Deal and even during the early days of Johnson's Great Society. This patriotic spirit arose from wide social agreement on the activities and endeavors of the federal government. Of course, each period, with the possible exception of the Great Society, involved an acute threat to the national welfare and survival. During the wars, the threat was foreign aggression, and during the New Deal, it was economic catastrophe. However, not all wars and military conflicts aroused a widespread patriotic passion. Korea hardly did. Vietnam definitely did not. While the country seemed to barely take notice of the more recent military involvements in Panama, Grenada, and Lebanon, patriotism roared back during the Gulf War.

There is much indication, however, that Americans desire a sense and feeling of patriotism that outlasts wars and national crises. This desire seemed evident after the Gulf War. America's military involvement naturally fired patriotic emotions, but when the conflict ended and America's eyes turned home to its domestic problems, many hoped that the patriotic intensity that supported the troops in the gulf could persist in the effort to combat drug violence, improve education, and reach racial harmony. Many Americans desired a patriotism that meant more than just standing up to Saddam Hussein – they seemed to yearn for a more enduring sense of the nation and a feeling of being part of an identifiable and unified community. Yet the only signs or barometers of patriotism, both before and after the war, seemed to exist in the national symbols and ideology. Indeed, the flag and the Pledge of Allegiance in recent years have appeared to be the only tangible signs of patriotism, and debates about censorship of speech criticizing those symbols have comprised most of the debates about patriotism.

Patriotism in the United States is more explicitly ideological and less land- or birth-oriented than is the case elsewhere. Unlike most other peoples, being an American is a matter of faith and conviction. The Japanese, for instance, do not commonly associate their identity with any national beliefs or convictions.

Patriots – the "true Americans" – have historically been identified by their commitment to the political values and symbols expressing the American ideology. Indeed, because the United States today remains a conglomeration of various groups who come together in an uneasy political relationship organized around the central force of liberal democracy, a sense of patriotism often exists only in the expression of ideological values.

The search for a meaning of patriotism therefore necessarily involves the national speech and symbols. In a fundamental way, patriotism is the words and description of a nation; and, like individuals, a nation derives a significant part of its identity from what is said about it. Thus, the censorship battles of the 1920s and 1950s over speech espousing socialist or Communist ideas reflected a struggle to define American patriotism and the symbols of national identity.

The most recent incidents of patriotism-inspired censorship arose in the 1988 election, with the question of mandated recitation of the Pledge of Allegiance in schools and the controversy over the flag-burning issue. Those rallying behind the flag saw it as a symbol of national unity and patriotism, even if that symbol is rather ambiguous. Senator Trent Lott, in explaining his support of a constitutional amendment to prohibit flag-burning, decried "a lack of appreciation for important symbols"; and Congressman Newt Gingrich said, "It's a very real issue because symbols matter."[13]

Though symbols matter, the question is what they signify. For instance, were the individuals who opposed the censorship inherent in the flag desecration law patriotic? Or were the patriots those who felt that citizenship should carry some mandate to respect and support certain symbols of national identity? This question also carried over to the patriotism of the Gulf War protesters. Were they, who acted in memory of the country's mistakes in Vietnam, patriotic in their opposition to the war? And likewise, are those who stress a unified view of society patriotic, or are the patriots those who recognize and support a multicultural view?

Despite these questions over the meaning of patriotism, however, the mere existence of national symbols carries a certain patriotic spirit, even if those symbols are vague and undefined. At least the existence of national symbols might suggest a unity that may not altogether exist in reality. It is this illusion of symbols that the censorship movement behind the flag-burning amendment may have sought to maintain.

Recent patriotism-related censorship attempts, such as the flag-burning law, have reflected a striving for some consensus and unity. In a diverse society, only speech and symbols can provide such elements of unity and draw together people who otherwise have little in common.

In the midst of nagging domestic problems and increased racial and gender tension, it was not surprising that the Bush administration fiercely sought to preserve the flag as a symbol and embodiment of a national identity. National unity has been greatly eroded by callous individualism. And racial polarization has affected much of public life in America — turning cities, parks, and transit systems into racial combat zones. Thus, perhaps the Bush administration thought that the maintenance of a national symbol of unity would postpone the hard task of forging a real unity among the diverse segments of American society. Nations secure in their identities and confident in their purpose, as the United States has been at times in the past, do not usually feel the need to define patriotism by law or by fragile symbols.

A similar need for unity and security was revealed in the recent struggle of New York City police officers to wear flag patches on their uniforms. Oddly enough, this request was initially denied by the department because it would violate its strict uniform standards. The interesting point of this struggle, however, was that it so prominently occurred in a department that has faced so many divisive battles recently. Perhaps because the department has been so criticized for failure to curtail crime and has faced so much internal turmoil over racial diversity, the symbolic victory of the flag patches held so much force. Thus, as with the nation as a whole, the battle over the flag patches involved more than the question of uniform appearances: it involved a struggle to find some unifying or identifying force among a fragmented and diverse group of people.

Likewise, the battle over flag-burning involved a conflict over the national identity. Would America be defined by the traditionalists who defended the flag? Or would it be defined by the perceived cultural radicals who did the flag-burning? As one American Legion member said in denouncing the Court ruling that granted constitutional protection to anyone burning the flag in political protest, "I don't give a damn whether it's [the protestor's] civil right or not. I fought to protect the American flag, not to protect him."[14]

Symbols, as demonstrated by the flag controversy, possess great power in America. Such power results not just because so much of American history involves myth and symbols, but because America has become such a media society. The media, and particularly television, spread speech and symbols throughout society and often elevate them to national focus. The flag-burning controversy, for instance, arose from the act of one individual burning a flag at the 1984 Republican convention. Yet this single act of symbol desecration spread throughout society via the media, as if the act had occurred thousands of times in thousands of communities.

The media has come to form one of the most powerful common areas in American life. It often seems to be the only glue or bond in society. As this common bond, the media quickly becomes the process or the forum through which America is defined and identified, often through symbols. The tent of the modern media covers a greater proportion of the population than does any other tent of commonality. When, for instance, the tent of television goes up, millions of Americans gather and watch with a common vision. And so the temptation exists to control and censor the images and speech conveyed through this medium and thereby to create the illusion that the common audience makes up a common culture with a clear national identity.

Censorship campaigns in the context of national symbols like the flag can be a means to participate in the battle over American identity. Indeed, what has often united society has been a common enemy – and censorship crusades provide such an enemy in the form of the censored speech. At the present time, however, the battle over identity seems to be intensifying. One symptom of this battle is the presence and intensity of cultural issues in the political arena. Such issues as race and gender, abortion, and gay rights make up a cultural politics that is relatively new to the American experience. Along with a growing recognition of multiculturalism, these issues reflect a continuing but intensifying struggle to redefine America.

Another somewhat subtle sign of the struggle for national identity lies in the continuing pressures for adherence to mainstream thinking. The political arena has been particularly plagued with a forced conformity to ideas and speech of mainstream America. Both liberals and conservatives have been criticized for being outside the mainstream of thinking. Though the effect is to censor controversial and innovative thinking, this mainstream preoccupation perhaps results from the same desire to promote social unity and identity as does the movement to ban desecration of the flag. Essentially, the enforced orthodoxy and conformity of the mainstream standard illustrates yet another face of the struggle to define America.

This struggle, however, is a consistent chapter in the American story. Being an aggregation of nearly every race and ethnic origin on earth, America lacks the assured cultural definition of national identity that one finds in European nation-states. America, after all, is a chalkboard; it is always being written over. And speech is often the chalk, and censorship the eraser, that is used on that chalkboard.

As America seeks new cultural identity, the current censorship attempts have focused on symbolic and artistic speech more than on political or informative speech. As demonstrated by the obscenity trial involving the Mapplethorpe exhibit in Cincinnati and the effort to restrict the artistic activities of the National Endowment for the Arts, censorship has turned increasingly to artistic and cultural speech.[15] Consequently, art in the present age has become much more than just artistic expression; it has become politicized as a symbol of society.

In this realm of symbolic national identity, censorship may stem not simply from a reaction against individual freedom, but from a desire to create or control national symbols and identity. It is an attempt to create some commonality in a diverse culture, a desire to forge a common identity from a perceived advancing cult of ethnicity and separatism. It reflects a longing for some universal value system and for the sewing together of the diverse patches of American culture into a national quilt. It is the hope to forge a history of consensus rather than conflict.

Censorship can therefore be seen as part of the ongoing struggle for national identity. In seeking to censor flag-burning, for instance, the public is reacting against the perceived rejection of American identity and values. This loyalty to symbols is certainly not all that unusual. In more culturally homogeneous countries like Israel and the Arab states, any desecration of national symbols would never be permitted. Furthermore, religious denominations treat their symbols with worshipful reverence. Even fraternal organizations frequently have symbols that form an important part of their identity and that command universal respect of the members.

Yet, as much as censorship might be a natural reaction to a battle over identity, such censorship contradicts the American experience. Only free expression can accommodate the continual rewriting of the national identity. As it is also a symbol of society, however, the marketplace of public speech must mirror the nature of its society. Since

America is a multicultural society, its speech must also be diverse and multicultural.

Much of twentieth-century censorship has been a crusade to convince Americans that they do not live in a land of rich ethnic and regional diversity. It has tried to maintain the myth that America is one homogeneous culture. Unfortunately, however, this crusade has cut off the ethnic roots of many older immigrant groups and has also spawned a resentment against the ethnic and racial groups that currently insist on being recognized for their separate identity and culture. Indeed, the multicultural movement has revealed the dangers in a society pretending that it is a homogeneous one when it is not – dangers that include racism, conformity, and cultural schizophrenia.

Only through a tolerance and encouragement of a free marketplace of speech will the nation peacefully adapt to this identity that exists in reality, even if this diverse identity is not always recognized. Indeed, tolerating speech is the first step to tolerating diversity. It is also the key to preserving American liberty and social peace. As James Madison predicted, it is precisely the plurality of religious and cultural voices that has prevented the lasting dominance of any single group. Furthermore, censorship for the sake of defining what we love often can masquerade as a hatred and fear of what we do not know or of what is different. In this sense, censorship encourages not a positive form of patriotism and national identity but a negative and dark side of patriotic sentiment. And as such, it serves no legitimate patriotic purpose.

The fight over free speech and censorship throughout the twentieth century has frequently involved America's effort to define itself. Periods of social change and instability, during which the country has wrestled with its social identity, have characteristically witnessed the escalation of censorship activity. Although aiming to produce social unity, however, this kind of censorship can only provide a false sense of identity and security by muting the discordant voices in society.

The Last Option

When the constitutional framers drafted the Bill of Rights protecting freedom of speech, only two forms of speech existed: written and verbal. Written speech appeared in the small-scale book and newspaper publishing industries and in written correspondence between individuals. Verbal speech was likewise conducted on a fairly small-scale basis. With no audio technologies available, all verbal speech took place on the personal level. Across the dining table, in the garden, out on the soapbox, and in the debate halls were where the nonwritten communication in society transpired.

Communication in the eighteenth and nineteenth centuries occurred in predictable and self-contained arenas. If people did not open their doors to visitors, they received no news of the neighboring community. If one did not stop at the town square or village hall, he or she did not share in the social communication on the public concerns of the day. Speech thus required a willing and committed listener. Consequently, social communication was an easily confined and controlled function, especially since there were so few outlets and forums for it.

In the 1990s, however, social communication is neither so easily controlled nor so personal. Not confined to the soapbox or debate hall, and not easily confined to any particular audience, speech today is a constant and ever-present part of daily life. As electronic and telecommunication technologies continually increase the presence and influence of speech in everyday life, speech comes to be perceived more as a social action or a commodity than the communication of an idea.

This growing identification of speech as an action or a commodity significantly contributes to society's willingness and desire to censor. Censorship is viewed as necessary to combat the harmful or evil action caused by certain expressions. Perceived as a necessary social reaction, censorship is not seen to be the restriction on freedom of speech that it ultimately is. To understand the categorization of speech as action and the resulting effect on censorship attitudes, the nature and role of speech in a media society must be examined.

In a media society, speech is no longer a personal act of expression between individuals. Instead, it has been transformed into a kind of public commodity. It entertains society, sells products, and elects politicians. It visits individual homes constantly through the telephone, the television, the VCR, and the radio. Speech is packaged on the television, and it is timed and charged on the telephone. When the children have to do their homework, it becomes a distraction – something that needs to be turned off. Even when they have finished their studies, its advertisements become a temptation – something that needs to be avoided.

Through the mass media, speech has come to have a life of its own. Separated from the relationship of speaker and listener, media speech keeps going as long as the batteries run and the electricity flows. Rather than simply being the reflection of a communicating society, the modern media itself has in some ways replaced society. It does not just reflect what individuals are expressing about life, it becomes the actual subject of life. Television audiences live for their shows and schedule their time around the viewing of a televised imitation of life. When a popular program is cancelled or even temporarily replaced by a special news program, a storm of protest frequently erupts that can be more virulent than any political protest. For many, ratings on television programs have become more important news than most of what transpires in our streets and schools. Another all-important news item is the weekly announcement of gross revenues earned by the current line-up of motion pictures. Even political campaign reporting is directed more and more at the content of the various candidates' television ads and media strategies.

Television has become the common culture of the generations that have grown up with it. To Americans under the age of thirty, according to sociologist Todd Gitlin, television constitutes their collective dream machine and their sense of being members of a nation. While television used to be about big events like presidential elections and moon walks, it is now a basic ingredient in daily life.

In its modern role, television does more than communicate about life;

it becomes the activity of life. Viewing talk shows replaces conversing with one's neighbor. Instead of communicating about the day's events, a family on its evenings together may pull up a chair and begin silently watching. The activity of life is transferred from the town square to the television set, where most of the social communicating transpires today. Through the modern media, Americans have been turned into an audience, where they watch and listen to life. Thus, communication through the media becomes more of an act or a thing than the sharing of ideas between people.

Life in the media culture of the 1990s is experienced through the media, not just talked about in the media. As the media shapes and acts upon society, it becomes an actor within society and the medium through which individuals increasingly experience much of modern life. The public's involvement in politics, its fearful reaction to crime, and its participation in social recreation such as sports activities can all occur in front of a television set. Of course, the danger is that the media may bring experiences to us that we neither want nor consider appropriate. Recently, for instance, a San Francisco television station attempted to film an execution at San Quentin prison. The court denied this request and ruled that reporters could bring in to the execution only paper and pen as reporting devices.[1] The emotional impact of watching a live execution, it was feared, might convert the event from a simple reporting of facts into a more physical experience of the event. Thus, one of the effects and consequences of a media society is that the speech and images carried over the mass media take on more of the characteristics or appearance of action.

This perception of speech as an action or commodity has important implications for the occurrence of censorship attempts in contemporary society. As speech becomes identified as an action or commodity, censorship can occur without being categorized as a restraint on expression.

Speech through the modern media has taken on a much different form and has much greater influence than personal speech between individuals. It is elevated, at least in perception, to a much more powerful and influential role. The October 1990 trial of the rap group 2 Live Crew demonstrates this effect. The group stood trial in Florida on obscenity charges relating to a concert during which songs containing explicit, street-language references to sex acts were performed. Though the six-person jury included four white women whose ages ranged from forty-two to seventy-six, it acquitted the group after only two hours of deliberation. Despite the prosecution's belief that the jury would be repulsed by the group's lyrics, "most of the jurors couldn't restrain their laughter when excerpts from the album were played in open court."[2] When exposed to the lyrics on a more personal level, and when able to confront the musicians face-to-face, the jurors could see the humor and perhaps the insignificance of them. However, when people hear such lyrics on a more impersonalized level, they are more inclined to attach more significant and harmful consequences to them. Thus, by divorcing the identity of the speaker from the speech, the media can transform the message conveyed from a mere expression to a kind of media action or event. Moreover, through the media, speech can come to personify or embody the underlying act or event. As it epitomizes social conflicts, for example, flag-burning, it brings the reality of what is happening elsewhere in time and place into the home. This also helps transform speech into perceived action. For instance, television images of flag-burning or of abortion protesters can do more than convey the fact that a protest occurred—it can engulf the viewer into an emotional experience of the event and convince the viewer that the particular expression is occurring in her own neighborhood.

As modern society becomes more impersonal and disconnected, the media gradually becomes the only opportunity for involvement or interaction. The media, in effect, provides America's common national ground. With the public increasingly estranged from active and personal involvement in mass society and politics, the media assumes the role of reality surrogate. Consequently, speech often becomes the only outlet or opportunity for any action at all. And the action that occurs is frequently censorship.

Remedial action is obviously needed on America's serious social problems. Yet in this increasingly legalistic, complex, and bureaucratic world, responsive action by the public can be difficult to organize and direct. With most issues covered by organized professional lobbying or interest groups, the public often feels alienated or even unnecessary in any action on public issues. Even political campaigns are being conducted by professional consultants and fundraisers. The general public is relegated to licking envelopes.

As the issues become increasingly complicated, action is also inhibited because the direction and consequences of such action are unknown. Since the nation's health system, for instance, is directed by doctors and other health care professionals, it becomes almost impossible for the public to take intelligent action on a matter controlled by experts. And as the nation's race and gender relations become so strained and with little direction on how to reach a resolution, action by the public becomes bogged down in uncertainty, ideology, and bickering. Thus, because social action and reform are often so difficult to achieve, attention is turned instead to the control of speech expressing the social problems. Perhaps, for instance, activists try to censor racist speech because the problem of racism in society has proved to be so entrenched and so elusive of remedial action. Consequently, censorship arises as an attempt to deal with difficult and complex social problems that have seemingly remained impervious to change and resolution. The public turns to censorship as a tool of power out of a "sense of disappointment and frustration with formal politics."[3]

Discrimination and violence against women present such critical and complicated social problems that have not been sufficiently remedied by political action. Even though these problems have been well known for decades, there has been relatively slow and ineffective action toward correcting generations of discrimination. Given the difficulties and slowness of remedial action, impatient advocates turn to the symbols of the problem – speech. Thus, censorship often arises from a quick-fix mentality – from a belief that the fixing of speech will fix the underlying problem. And so pornography and politically incorrect speech are censored.

Given the quick-fix allure of censorship, it is tempting to equate verbal purification with genuine social reform. Yet even if all females are called women instead of girls, after "he" is not used to refer to all persons, and after all women are addressed as "Ms.," women will still only earn about two-thirds of what men earn. The only thing that censorship may actually accomplish is to hide the problem of sexual abuse and discrimination. The danger is that censorship, by making something secret, actually eroticizes that which is censored. Moreover, forbidden language may be dangerously attractive simply because it is forbidden.

Codes that regulate racist speech are also an attempt to take quick action on the symbol or reflection of an underlying social problem that has proved difficult to solve with remedial social action. The controversy and social divisiveness over affirmative action, for instance, demonstrate the difficulty of substantively addressing the problem of race discrimination. Therefore, speech symbolizing discrimination becomes the focus of the reformers' attention. Just as a sign in front of a building is easy to remove, speech reflecting discrimination is easy to identify and punish. But the building, just like the discrimination, remains.

Speech codes have been defended on the grounds that the speech they regulate rises to the level of socially harmful action. According to Stanley Fish, a professor of law and of English at Duke University, "It is right to ban the use of certain expressions likely to do things that cause trouble, [and] the risk of not attending to hate speech is greater than the risk of regulating it. "[4]

In taking a speech-control approach to address campus racial problems, Brown University recently passed a hate speech code that prohibits racial slurs or verbal harassment. Under this code, the university expelled a student for making offensive racial comments. Yet this punishment of speech reflects a quick-fix mentality directed only at the symptoms of a problem, which in reality requires far broader substantive remedial measures. According to Robert O'Neil, director of the Thomas Jefferson Center for the Protection of Free Expression, "Universities implement speech codes out of a sense of desperation and as a last resort when other approaches prove inadequate."[5] The end result of Brown University's censorship of racist speech may be simply to drive prejudiced attitudes underground, rather than to uproot them. Although such well-meaning censorship may strive to eliminate problems of racism, sexism, and the like, it ultimately serves to hide those problems from public view, allowing them to fester and worsen.

Censorship as the surrogate for social action often occurs because there is more equality in speech power than in economic or political power. If a social problem involves the opposition of centers of economic and political power—for example, corporations—the public often does not have sufficient power to directly confront the problem. Speech then becomes the only apparent way to fight that problem.

Instances of such censorship often involve advertising. The Reverend Michael Pfleger, a priest in the South Side of Chicago, has led a long fight against billboards that advertise cigarettes, beer, and liquor in black and Hispanic neighborhoods. He criticizes cigarette makers, brewers, and distillers for targeting minority communities, where rates of smoking- and alcohol-related diseases are higher than in white communities. To combat this problem, Pfleger censors the billboard advertisements by covering them with red paint. Though he cannot fight the economic and political power of the tobacco and brewing corporations, Pfleger's campaign against their speech requires only enough economic resources to purchase a can of spray paint.

Pfleger is just one of many community activists across the country who wage censorship crusades against billboards they call twenty-four-hour pushers. The Reverend Calvin Butts leads a Harlem crusade against such billboard advertisers. In defending his crusade against advertising, Butts has argued that he "do[es] not believe that First Amendment rights give people license to say or do things that seriously harm others."

Advertisers, however, claim that these antibillboard activists are trying to restrict commercial speech protected by the First Amendment. Yet this campaign against commercial speech may be the only action available to social activists. Though the activists clearly do not possess the political power to outlaw the particular products nor the economic power to run the advertisers out of business, they do possess the power to censor the speech used to sell cigarettes and alcohol.

Likewise, in an effort to protect the environment, several states have attacked certain kinds of environmental advertising. In May 1991, eleven state attorneys general issued a report entitled "Recommendations for Responsible Environmental Advertising." In it, the state officials advocate regulation of the way in which environmental claims or statements can be made by manufacturers. Essentially, the report tries to tell manufacturers how to advertise the environmental aspects of their products. Critics of this report claimed that it was "replete with calls for self-censorship" and that it was really aimed at "environmentally incorrect speech."[6] Nonetheless, the report is another example of using the easier alternative of censorship when the remedial action needed to accomplish the desired social goals is both difficult and complex. Though the intent is the correction of an important social problem — pollution — the action taken is aimed solely at speech. Because, unlike pollution, environmentally incorrect speech can be quickly and definitively remedied through censorship.

Another example of such speech-focused reform, or censorship, is the call by the American Academy of Pediatrics for a ban on television junk-food ads. Their plea rests on evidence revealing that a single Saturday morning of TV cartoons contained 202 junk-food ads. The proposed ad ban aims at combating obesity and high cholesterol and improving the health of children. Parents have also joined in this plea — an act that perhaps reflects parental beliefs that the media has at times become the mainstream culture in their children's lives and may, even more than parents, influence and shape their children's behavior. Thus, parents have attempted to combat this health problem and the even larger problem of child-rearing with the only action available — censorship. Perhaps in this way parents feel they can begin to equalize the disparity in power between themselves and the media.

Advertising in political campaigns has also come under censorship pressures. As with crusades against other types of advertising, the reaction against political advertising reflects a frustration with much deeper and more complex problems concerning the political process. By prohibiting political advertising on television, campaign reformers hope to eliminate the need to raise large campaign funds and therefore to end the financial influence of special interests, to make politics more responsive to the average voter, and to elevate the debased political discourse that emerges from the contrived slogans and superficialities of campaign advertising. Yet censoring such advertising, though it may be easier to accomplish than the kind of reforms needed to reinvigorate democratic politics, will not suddenly achieve election reform, even if it does initially suppress some of the more bothersome symptoms of the problems with the political process.

Interestingly, most of these censorship crusades against advertising have been conducted by liberals. This pattern once again refutes the traditional explanation of censorship as the work of reactionary conservatives opposed to freedom. It also demonstrates that many liberals are addressing the power inequality in society by attacking the symbols or expression of that power. Or perhaps these liberals have decided that speech lies at the source of the problems and that by combating speech they can remedy the real problems like racism, pollution, and child nutrition.

The linkage of speech with action produces a strong tendency toward censorship. If speech is viewed as a commodity or an action, it can then be counteracted with action – the action of censorship. The importance of this association of speech with action and its consequent effect on censorship is further heightened by the fact that it often works through persons who traditionally do not advocate censorship. The opponents of certain kinds of advertising or racist speech, for instance, are striving not for the restriction of individual freedom but for the improvement of social conditions. By categorizing speech as action, they need not confront the full implications of their attempts at censorship.

Unfortunately, speech sometimes falls victim to our desire to act and to fix – and in that way speech becomes confused with action. Take, for instance, the efforts of some communities to fight prejudice through the passage of laws prohibiting hate speech. The St. Paul, Minnesota, city council in 1989 passed an ordinance that outlawed the placing on public or private property of any symbol or object "which one knows or has reasonable grounds to know arouses anger, alarm or resentment in others on the basis of race, color, creed or religion." As explained by St. Paul Mayor Jim Scheibel, the law was enacted because "like other cities, we were seeing more racially motivated and religion-oriented crimes."[7] As seen by supporters of the law, it addressed deplorable conduct and acts of violence, and so it did not infringe on free speech. Consequently, freedom-loving liberals could agree on regulation of such speech, because it was not even seen as speech. Just as the patriots of revolutionary America believed that the only free speech was the speech of freedom, thus justifying their censorship of pro-British sentiment, so too do the advocates of hate speech censorship believe that the only free speech is that which does not offend or arouse anger or fear in others.

Restrictions on hate speech have also become a popular response to expressions of racism on college campuses. Almost two hundred universities have implemented such speech codes.[8] These codes, however, have blurred the distinction between offensive conduct and offensive ideas. And in trying to combat the former, they have focused on the latter.

Speech can be like a weed in the lawn. It is easier and temporarily gratifying to cut it down, but without pulling out the roots the weed still lives and grows. So too with speech: though it may be easier to censor offensive speech, such censorship will not pull out the roots of the underlying problem. Action must be addressed with action, and speech with speech. Racist speech must be answered with enlightened speech, and racism must be answered with justice. As Justice Louis Brandeis said in 1927, "The remedy to be applied is more speech, not enforced silence."[9] Free expression is needed to reveal the social problems, just as the leaves of the weed are needed to show the location of its roots.

The more that speech becomes intermingled with action, the more it rises to the level of action and becomes vulnerable to the regulatory action of censorship. One way in which speech is linked with action occurs when the public believes that certain speech can lead to or incite certain activity. An example of this perceived relationship lies in the area of pornographic and sexist speech.

Pornographic and sexually explicit speech have historically been the subject of censorship crusades. While most of these crusades have been initiated by those attempting to uphold traditional moral and religious values, the current crusade has an additional motivation and different leaders. According to the new proponents of censorship, pornographic speech should be censored because it leads to discrimination and violence against women. Although the actual linkage of speech and action is highly disputed, the censorship advocates do cite their evidence.

One study found that child molesters and rapists used pornography more than nonoffenders.[10] Likewise, sociologists Larry Baron and Murray Straus reported in the December 1987 issue of *Social Problems* that states that have a higher number of rapes per capita also have higher circulation rates of sex magazines. They concluded that even soft-core pornography helps create an environment ripe for rape.[11] In an article published in 1988 in *The Journal of Personality and Social Psychology*, researchers from the University of California and the University of Wisconsin reported that men who watched sexually violent films showed less concern about violence against women than men who did not.[12] According to three other researchers who wrote for *The Journal of Research in Personality* in 1988, men who used sexually violent material expressed a greater likelihood of committing rape or using sexual force against women than men who did not use pornography. The U.S. attorney general's Commission on Pornography was even more definitive. Its 1986 report stated that a direct causal relationship existed between exposure to pornography and violence against women.

These findings and conclusions, however, are contradicted in many other studies.[13] Nonetheless, the possibility of a linkage, along with the dramatic growth in recent years of pornographic material, has prompted many persons to advocate censorship as a response to the increasing violence against women.[14] Given the seriousness of this problem, the desire to take some definitive action with definitive results is obviously tempting. Censorship provides such a temptation, particularly since the psychological and sociological mysteries of the causes of violence against women render any other remedial action difficult to implement. Because the speech of pornography and sexism has been linked to action and violence, the restriction of such speech is not seen as censorship but as a necessary remedial action.[15]

A similar attitude applies to recent efforts to ban nude dancing and television violence. The Supreme Court recently overturned Indiana's public indecency law that prohibited the display of male or female genitals and buttocks. This case arose from the efforts of residents of South Bend, Indiana to eliminate nude dancing at local clubs and bars. These efforts, however, stem from more than just a moral objection to nude dancing—they arise from an attitude that such expressions constitute conduct that is threatening the community. As Deputy Attorney General Wayne Uhl said in defending the indecency law, people appearing naked in public is the kind of conduct that "promotes prostitution, encourages sexual assault . . . and leads to conduct such as adultery and divorce that breaks down the family structure."[16] South Bend residents also explained their opposition to nude dancing as their desire to clean up their community and as their belief that dancing was conduct and not speech.

Censorship of television depictions of violence is also motivated by the perception that media violence is having a dangerous effect on viewers, particularly youth. The ever-increasing depiction of violence on television is considered by many to be creating a modern culture of violence. According to some psychologists and media critics, the constant exposure of boys to so-called adventure films, which are often in reality nonstop violence films, makes those boys more prone to violent activity. By the time American youths are eighteen years old, according to social philosopher Myriam Miedzian, they have watched twenty-six thousand murders on television alone.

The assumption that media-depicted violence is a component or instigator of violent behavior leads many to advocate much more serious restrictions on television and movie content. Yet those restrictions are not perceived as a reaction against speech, but as a crusade against violence in society. Thus, as violent speech is equated with violent behavior, censorship of the former becomes much more understandable as a reaction against the latter, rather than as an intolerance of free expression.

This campaign against violent movies and television programs also mirrors a campaign against heavy metal and rap lyrics, which also are seen to encourage rape and bigotry. Actions taken against rap groups including 2 Live Crew and N.W.A. have been justified as necessary to combat violence encouraged by the violent and sexually explicit language of the groups' lyrics. As one state attorney general explained his state's attempt to ban sales of the N.W.A. album to minors, "The issue here is not record-burning or censorship, [it] is the access by minors to harmful and sexually offensive material."[17] Rap music, however, is not the only music subject to contemporary censorship attempts. Warner Brothers Records, for instance, pulled from radio stations and video outlets the country music song "Maybe I Mean Yes" by Holly Dunn because of the perception that it could encourage date rape.

A recent trial of the rock group Judas Priest also reflects the growing impulse to censor messages that become equated with violent actions. The group was tried in 1990 on an accusation that the lyrics in "Better by You, Better than Me" had led two Nevada youths to kill themselves. As attorneys for the group argued, "Artists cannot be held entirely responsible for actions some listeners may take after hearing their records."[18]

Perhaps the most vehement and determined public outcry against rap lyrics expressing violence occurred in the summer of 1992 in connection with the song "Cop Killer" performed by Ice-T. In that song, Ice-T shouts "Die, pig, die" and chants of being " 'bout to dust some cops off." The ensuring public outrage and boycott of the album's distributor, Time Warner, convinced the company to discontinue its distribution of "Cop Killer." Although the record company had defended the song on the basis of First Amendment concerns, the song's opponents denied that the matter was a free speech issue. Instead, they argued that it was a violence-as-entertainment issue.[19]

Other examples of censorship based on the linkage of speech with action include New York's "Son of Sam" law, which prohibited publishers from paying advances and royalties to persons convicted of crimes who later write books about those crimes.[20] The law was intended to remove any financial reward or compensation from persons who committed crimes and then wrote books about those crimes. Thus, the words of the criminal become linked with the acts of the criminal. In another attempt to address social problems through action against speech, or perhaps just as an attempt to cover up a problem, New York City recently banned all forms of begging in the city's subway system.[21]

Although the increasing tendency to view speech as action has primarily occurred in relation to certain social problems, it has also arisen in relation to the concept of image that became so important and pervasive during the 1980s. According to many social critics, that decade was characterized by an obsession with image. Success in business did not depend on quality products, it depended on glitzy marketing and sales campaigns. The image of a product was more important than its quality. Likewise, politicians became more concerned with their image than with the votes they were making on specific issues. Indeed, it seemed as if everyone wanted her share of the social spotlight or, as Andy Warhol predicted, his fifteen minutes of fame.

The creation of image became an all-consuming national obsession. This image, however, was a product of media portrayal. Consequently, the concern for image translated into a desire to control the expressions in the media. In addition, the concern for reputation also influenced attitudes toward speech.

Reputation in early American society was something personal. It was formed as a result of how the community viewed and interacted with an individual. However, as American society became more of a media society and as the communal bonds and networks weakened, reputation became more impersonal.

People now acquire a public reputation, not through individual relationships, but through publicity. This public reputation or media image becomes the social identity of the person. It is in this area that a new kind of censorship arises. As social status rests on image and appearance, and since speech creates image, the molding or censoring of speech is simply a matter of molding one's image in a society that encourages such molding.

The boom of gossip columnists and celebrity journalism during the 1980s demonstrated the importance of image in a media society and revealed an increasing obsession with media reputation.[22] The nation became preoccupied with the lives of the image-makers and the rich and famous. President Reagan and his "Teflon presidency" also reflected this concern with image. Social commentators described a new class in the American social scene—a nouveau celebrity class applauded less for achievement than for the mere act of becoming famous.

Because of this concern with image, the media became the battleground of individual reputation and identity. Censorship by libel ensued, as libel actions by disgruntled media subjects proliferated. The 1980s witnessed a libel explosion. According to the Libel Defense Resource Center, the average libel award against media defendants in the two-year period from 1989 to 1990, an average of almost $4.5 million, was ten times higher than during the previous two-year period.[23] However, these libel lawsuits, such as the ones brought by well-known public figures like Wayne Newton and General Westmoreland, which are themselves widely publicized in the media, may be more attempts to mold media reputation than to win money awards through lawsuits. Thus, speech becomes a battleground of image, not a marketplace of ideas as envisioned by Justice Holmes.

It is not just libel plaintiffs and image-conscious publicity seekers who try to censor speech distasteful to them. In a society focused on media image, many types of persons and groups resort to censorship activities in an effort to shape their image. Some feminists, for instance, seek to eliminate the type of fashion magazines that they say reinforce the image of women as sex objects. Mary Lynn Naughton, manager of the University of Dayton bookstore, refused to carry the swimsuit edition of *Sports Illustrated,* arguing that the magazine "exploits and objectifies women."[24] African-Americans also object to images in the media, such as depictions of black youths as criminals, that project an undesirable impression. Such books as *The Merchant of Venice, Oliver Twist, Little Black Sambo,* and *The Adventures of Huckleberry Finn* have received censorship pressures from Jews and African-Americans who claim that the books perpetuate racial stereotypes. The novel *To Kill a Mockingbird* and the movie *Fort Apache, The Bronx* have also been accused of depicting African-Americans in a racist light. And during the 1991 World Series, Native Americans objected to the name of one of the participating teams—the Atlanta Braves—and to various Indian-style chants used by fans during the games. Such names and chants, according to the protestors, create a negative image of Native Americans. As one Native American protestor explained, "[W]e're not mascots, [w]e're human beings."[25]

The problem of the wrong or misused language, to many minority groups, is that it builds social stereotypes. Thus, image is no longer a reflection of reality; in a media society it becomes a controller and determinant of reality. As such, a component of image—speech—takes on an identity and meaning other than merely the expression of ideas. Consequently, censorship can appear to its advocates not as a reaction against freedom of speech, but as a necessary tool for image enhancement and social standing.

The view of speech held by the image-censors is that language controls reality. Yet the linguist Joshua Whatmough has argued in his book, *Language: A Modern Synthesis,* that language use follows reality and does not control it. Nonetheless, the current wave of image censorship demonstrates the pervasiveness of the belief that by changing language it is possible to change reality. This role of speech is reflected in the beliefs of the Czech leader and playwright Vaclav Havel, who has spoken of the miracle of speech as emancipatory and of the power of words to change history.[26]

The flip-side of image, and a similarly significant contributor to censorship motivations, is the concern for privacy. This concern, like image, results from the media prevalence in society. As the media increasingly publicizes the private sides of individual lives, the concern for privacy and for protection from the media rises in intensity. Just as speech can be a shaper and determinant of image, so too can it be an intrusion into privacy. Media intrusions, such as the one involving the man who stopped the attempted assassination of President Ford and whose gay lifestyle was later exposed by the press, can be more damaging than the intrusion of a burglar into one's home. And unlike the precautions we can take to keep a burglar out, there are few precautions people can take to keep the media out of their lives. Thus, speech that invades privacy comes to be seen less as expression and more as an act of intrusion. Consequently, as in other areas previously mentioned, censorship again is seen more as a reaction to undesirable action than as a restriction of free speech. In the area of privacy, the concern is not over speech but over intrusions.

Privacy censorship is occurring today through an increasing number of lawsuits alleging invasion of privacy. In addition to these lawsuits, other types of privacy censorship attempts are taking place. Recently, for instance, NASA refused to release to the media an audio tape of the last moments of the astronauts who died aboard the space shuttle Challenger. It claimed that such a release would disclose personal information that may invade the privacy of the astronauts and their families. Reacting to other kinds of privacy fears, Congress and the FCC have moved to regulate caller identification and automatic dialing telephone services.

Privacy has also become a primary concern in rape cases. A recent Gallup survey showed that nearly nine out of ten people believe that reporting the name of a woman who has been raped constitutes "a special hardship for women."[27] Many experts claim that disclosure of the name of a rape victim has a chilling effect on the reporting of rape crimes to the police. Thus, the media's disclosure of the identity of the victim is seen not only as an invasion of privacy but as an act that hampers the fight against rape in society. This view of speech as action prevailed during a recent debate over a bill in the Iowa state legislature to prevent the police from releasing the names of rape victims until after an arrest has been made. As one of the supporters and lobbyists for the bill explained, "[A]ll the bill does is give a victim a little time to deal with what has happened to her, for her to tell her husband and family, [i]t has nothing to do with censorship."[28]

As society comes to value privacy more, it will take more aggressive action against intrusions into that privacy. The development of new communications technologies also threatens to raise greater concerns for privacy. For instance, telecommunications technologies that permit fundraisers various forms of access to individual telephone subscribers' homes obviously affect privacy concerns. Indeed, because of new technologies and the highly developed media industries, the zone of privacy is increasingly becoming associated with a zone of speech, rather than the physical zone of the home. While we can shut the door to outside visitors, we cannot shut the door of our homes to public expression through the various forms of the media. Consequently, speech can become more the visitor we do not want than the embodiment of ideas we can debate.

As speech continues to take an ever more prominent role in our media society, the view of it as something more than it is – something like a commodity or an action – becomes increasingly popular, and hence increasingly contributes to occurrences of censorship. Yet such censorship of speech in the name of action is ultimately self-defeating, because it inhibits any real action on the underlying social problems. Action requires speech. If problems cannot be freely discussed or revealed through speech, they cannot be solved.

Communication is the key to addressing most problems. Experts have found, for instance, that children who can communicate with their parents are less likely to use drugs. Surely, then, it is not in the interest of drug abuse prevention for parents to inhibit the expressions of any troubles or concerns their children might have relating to drug use. So too it is with society. Open communication on all social problems is the key to solving them. As the history of social reform in America has shown, the more the actual social problems are addressed, the less the need to curtail speech.[29] The free expression of ideas constitutes the most important requirement for action. This realization was recently demonstrated by a group traditionally in favor of censorship. In its efforts to abolish the National Endowment for the Arts, a Christian lobbying group petitioned the FCC to get television stations to air explicit photographs funded by the NEA.[30]

The danger continually exists that censorship undertaken for the sake of reform may lead to a censorship of reaction. If minority groups, for instance, advocate censorship of books they claim depict them in an unfavorable light, they open the door to a reactive censorship against books that deal positively with those groups. If African-Americans succeed in censoring *The Adventures of Huckleberry Finn*, they make it more possible that *Soul on Ice* and *Best Short Stories by Negro Writers* can also be censored. The Minnesota Civil Liberties Union found, for instance, that in 1982 *Roots* had been banned in eighty-eight of the state's 235 school districts. Likewise, feminists should be wary of censorship of pornography. For without free speech the feminist movement would have encountered far more obstacles. Some feminists advocating censorship of sexually explicit materials may have forgotten that antiobscenity efforts have been trained regularly on *Our Bodies, Our Selves*.

Though undertaken in the name of social reform, censorship ultimately imposes a mandated conformity. It reflects an intolerant wish to cleanse the world of its imperfections and impurities, as seen by the censors. It attempts to dictate to society what is proper and enlightened. In an often impatient and hypersensitive world, censorship seeks to narrow the boundaries of the range of differences that must be tolerated. It expresses a meddling impulse to constantly fix and fine-tune society to the desires of the censors. And in so doing, censorship eventually drains society of its vitality, its diversity, and its spontaneity.

7

Quality through Censorship

Throughout the year people collect information on mutual funds in which they might invest at the end of the year. The file naturally starts out empty, but it quickly fills as everything that might be remotely useful is placed into it, even though most of the documents are never read beforehand. This indiscriminate filing continues throughout the year. Not surprisingly, by the end of the year the file is unmanageably thick. And the first task in reviewing the contents is always to throw away, to clean out the file as much as possible. Otherwise, there is too much information to digest. People can only use a certain amount – everything beyond that only seems to confuse and clutter our thinking.

So too, perhaps, does censorship function – as a file cleaner of the speech we think clutters our world. Throughout most of history we have taken the filing approach to information: the more the better. During the eighteenth, nineteenth, and early twentieth centuries, the increase in information was fairly manageable. In the modern information age, however, the increase has been phenomenal. With the corresponding expansion of the media, it is almost as if all the information has come out of the file drawer and is swirling around in the office of society.

Although America's steel production may have declined in recent decades, its information production has exploded. The libraries are bulging. To store all the information, microfilm and computer discs are

necessary – and even those are quickly filling the shelves. To accommodate and process this knowledge, college directories list hundreds of
courses offered in any one semester and bookstores keep building their
shelves higher and their aisles narrower.

Along with the increase of information, the means of communicating
that information have similarly expanded. Through the daily mail
come bundles of unsolicited letters and advertisements. In addition to
the mail, a multitude of delivery companies have been formed to trans-
port the ever increasing volume of documents and correspondence
passed within society. Newspaper and magazine racks displaying current periodicals fill entire library rooms – indeed, no bookstore could afford to carry them all. If a person tires of reading, however, she can
spend her time flipping through the array of cable stations received on
one of her television sets. Or she can converse on the telephone in her
car, transmit documents over her facsimile machine, or listen to one of
her hundreds of compact discs.

Perhaps all this information, particularly as it is distributed through
society by the media, produces a certain dulling or drowning effect.
Though knowledge can lead to progress and wisdom, it can only do so if
it can be understood, contemplated, and processed. Too much information, like too much food, can cause one to turn away from the table of
thought.

Individuals can hardly keep up with so much information. Not even
all the information that gets delivered to one's door gets read – the un-
touched magazines and journals, the unopened mail, and the unread
newspapers eventually build a pile of unfulfilled good intentions. Add
to this unconsumed information all the radio programs that get missed
and the public television specials that go unwatched. And then there is
the steady stream of new books that would look so good stacked next
to all the old ones still waiting for that rainy day. Indeed, people seem
to be constantly swimming against the tide of knowledge accumula-
tion. Yet if they cannot consume this knowledge, if they cannot sift out
the truly valuable pieces of information, all the information in the
world is useless to them. Eventually, the widening gulf between available information and consumed information results only in frustration.

As the information age coincides with the media and technology age,
the effect of the knowledge overflow is two-fold. First, the increase in
information outpaces society's ability to process and evaluate it. Second, through publication by the pervasive media, the increase in information is readily and immediately apparent. The information flood is
reflected and even magnified by the constant waves of speech. With the
speed of modern communication technologies, information and ideas
are exchanged without allowing the time that once existed to reflect
and adjust to that information. Inevitably, this inability to adjust in-

creases the temptation to turn to simple methods to control or limit the communication of information, even though such communication may once have been valued as the exercise of free speech.

Many people in society are reacting to the information explosion by attempting to clean out the clutter of information, to sift through the overwhelming amount of knowledge that is being produced in the information age. As publishers have realized, newspaper readership is stagnating and general interest magazines such as *Look* have disappeared. People are looking for ways to narrow their focus to only a small and manageable range of information. Executives demand one- or two-page summary memos. News programs try to capsulize the day's news into one half-hour segment. Indeed, the sound-bite may be as much a reflection of the desire to simplify as it is a product of the cost of broadcast time in the modern media. Thus, even as the amount of information is skyrocketing, society is just as rapidly trying to sort out and throw away all but the most essential information.

Since speech is the transmitter of information, the attempt to sort out the usable information from the unusable may be yet another motivation behind the censorship impulse in contemporary society. This kind of censorship involves a perception that too much information exists and that some quality screening should occur. Since speech is a barometer or reflection of information, censorship consequently indicates a social desire to impose some quality control and to simplify the overwhelming amount of information in society.

Underlying this concept of censorship is the notion that restricting the already overabundant speech does not really eliminate or suppress any worthwhile ideas, which are probably expressed elsewhere and in better form. Censorship is merely a throwing out of all the unnecessary clutter or excess of speech. Like cleaning up the streets of the city, censorship acts like the street-cleaner of the public forum of speech. As Paul Fussell writes in *Bad: Or, The Dumbing of America*, the primary public discourse in modern society is that of advertising and publicity, and the language itself is corrupt and debased. It was perhaps with this realization and with the desire to separate the bad speech from the good that the Quincy, Massachusetts, city council recently passed an ordinance banning any swearing in public places. With a similar intent to eliminate the clutter of obscenity from public speech, the Justice Department in 1989 increased their obscenity prosecutions 400 percent from the previous year, which had followed a 100 percent increase from 1987.

The impulse to censor resulting from a perceived clutter of unnecessary speech does not inherently strive to completely eliminate certain speech—it just tries to organize or separate it. Just as zoning laws try to confine or organize certain kinds of buildings, censorship may try to organize the haphazard clutter of speech. Advocates for the censorship of television programming, for instance, do not seek to totally ban adult programs and language – they just want to move such programming to certain cable channels. The mayor of a town that censored the movie *The Cook, the Thief, His Wife, and Her Lover* explained this organizational approach to censorship: "I can understand if you show it in New York City. I can even understand if you show it in Dallas, Texas. But this is a suburban community of families [and] no place for an X-rated movie."[1]

This organizational or quality-control aspect of censorship reflects a fear that too much information is being communicated and that too much of the information is irritating at best and destructive at worst. For social knowledge to advance, ways must be found to eliminate the distraction of worthless information. Consequently, various contemporary censorship crusades reflect a social attitudinal shift away from quantity and toward quality of the information communicated in the marketplace of ideas.

Underlying the recent campaign to restrict the kinds of art funded by the NEA, for instance, was a desire to impose some quality standards on publicly funded art and to establish some standard of artistic value. Public opinion polls reflect this popular notion of censorship as an acceptable method of imposing quality controls. A survey conducted by the Thomas Jefferson Center for the Protection of Free Expression revealed that, while Americans overwhelmingly believe that the Constitution protects their right of free speech, more than 25 percent said that such protections should not apply to the arts or the media. In a poll commissioned by People for the American Way, 53 percent of the survey group thought that art should be censored if it offended a majority of the public.[2] Thus, according to large numbers of people, censorship can be used to clean up bad art.

A quality consciousness toward speech has inspired several recent public reactions against what is perceived as bad art or literature. One such reaction came against Bret Easton Ellis's novel *American Psycho*. When Simon & Schuster decided against publishing this novel, which involved a main character gruesomely depicted as demented and violent against women, children, and street beggars, cries of censorship arose from the Authors Guild. Yet the decision not to publish the book more likely resulted from a conclusion that the book was repulsive and disgusting in its message. Simon & Schuster's decision provoked no great public concern for free speech or the dangers of censorship, perhaps because the public wondered why the book should be allowed to be published, to occupy valuable space on crowded bookshelves, and to consume the pulp of large numbers of increasingly scarce trees, when so many other good books are available to publish and distribute.

Similarly, the public support of the Reverend Jerry Falwell's position in *Hustler v. Falwell*, a case in which Falwell sued *Hustler* magazine for publishing a parody ad that portrayed Falwell as a drunkard whose first sexual experience was with his mother in an outhouse, reflected such an outrage against disgusting speech. Likewise, there were public reactions against Andrew Dice Clay and his outflow of dirty words; the book *Modern Primitives*, which depicted genitals split and mutilated with pins and punctured by rings, and against the sculpture the University of the District of Columbia tried to buy for $1 million that depicted thirty-nine place settings of the artist's interpretation of a vulva on a plate. Even modern literature has attracted quality-conscious objections. Consider, for instance, the criticisms of the anthology of short stories and poetry entitled *The Quarterly, Summer 1990* published by Random House. This anthology includes stories of incest—a boy kissing his mother and a daughter sexually impaling herself on her father, a poem about a boy who wets his pants, a story about a woman who keeps sneezing in the direction of her husband—"I felt it all over, dampening my hair and dripping down my forehead and wetting my eyebrows, all these prickles of gooey snot sticking to my cheek and chin"—and a cartoon of oral sex.

With the increasing amounts of speech in society, perhaps Americans are reacting against the ugly speech, particularly since there seems to be so much ugliness in public speech. Indeed, to be noticed in the 1990s, it seems that artists and writers need to be shocking in their language and message. Anything but ugly risks being judged as simply bland and boring.

During the image-conscious period of recent years, in which notoriety and social attention were the ultimate status symbols, the shocking and the ugly often received the public eye. Yet as censorship attempts increased in response, they were attributed to the traditional forces of social intolerance and antilibertarianism. Very likely, however, these censorship attempts were instead motivated by a desire to make quality and aesthetic judgments, to clear away the ever-increasing amount of ugly speech and to find the valuable and worthwhile. As U.S. District Judge Dickran Tevrizian explained the removal of a sculpture showing a woman squatting and a baby girl lying on her back with legs open, both figures showing genitals, from the front of a new federal office building: "It's not censorship, [it] is bad taste art."[3]

Through censorship, the public often seeks to proclaim its judgment on the quality and value of art. After all, as Lyndon Johnson declared when he signed the law creating the NEA in 1965, "Art is a nation's most precious heritage." While a decision as to the quality of art is every person's individual right to make, unfortunately in America almost all decisions and controversies, even artistic ones, turn into political questions. Clearly, every taxpayer has a right to have a say about how her tax dollars are spent. Yet there is a fine line between discussing the federal funding of such agencies as the NEA and determining the kind of art that can be selected for sponsorship by such government agencies.

Likewise, there is a fine line between censorship and taste. For instance, the art of Andres Serrano and Jock Sturges raised much opposition, but the question is whether that opposition constitutes censorship or legitimate quality judgments. Serrano is best known for "Piss Christ," his image of a plastic crucifix in a tank of urine, and became something of an art-world hero for having provoked considerable ire from conservative Christian groups. Jock Sturges received much attention for his photographs of nude adolescents. As was true in the controversies surrounding the Mapplethorpe exhibit, the defenders of Serrano's and Sturges's First Amendment freedoms seemed reluctant to discuss artistic values. They saw censorship only as an attack on freedom, not as an attempted statement about the quality of publicly funded art. This labeling of every criticism as oppressive censorship, however, ignores the distinction between censuring and censoring. To censor is to eliminate speech, but to censure is to criticize certain speech and to form judgments about the quality of that speech. Though a free society must refrain from censoring, an enlightened society must never refrain from censuring.

Unfortunately, the politicization of artistic questions often replaces any quality concerns with the single legal issue of censorship. Yet quality objections to many art exhibits, as with the Serrano and Sturges exhibits, underlie various attempts at censorship. Consider, for instance, the objections to the NEA-funded photography of David Wojnarowicz, which included, among others, images of a man licking a cow's rectum and of Jesus Christ shooting up heroin. Attempted censorship of this kind of art may be the result of a groping social desire to improve the quality of public art and discourse – a desire that, like so many other disputes, inevitably ends up in the political arena.

This quality-motivated censorship may also underlie the efforts to control the public messages and information to which youth are exposed. With so many valuable books, why expose children to ones considered worthless or even disgusting? As a child's formal education occupies only a few hours of the days of a few years of an entire life, the choice of the right books and educational materials assumes a certain urgency. Consequently, the need to sift through all of the worthless and unnecessary books contributes to the impulse to censor school libraries and educational materials. Parents in Kankakee, Illinois, for instance, recently presented to school officials a list of textbooks to which they objected. According to the parents, the books "undermined truth and value" and taught "a curiosity in the occult."[4] Indeed, the number of censorship attacks on school books increased by 40 percent from 1989 to 1990, with frequently cited reasons for such censorship being satanism and dirty words.[5] Perhaps the most besieged of all school books is the *Impressions* reading series, which has come under attack from parents who think the series contains too many negative stories, too many witches, and too many references to Satanism.[6] With so much useful and necessary knowledge to pass on to children, advocates of censorship question the value of devoting educational resources to the topic of Satanism.

The realization that youth today are subjected to so much more information and speech and that parents have less ability in a media society to control the information received by their children has also inspired efforts to censor the media messages that youth receive outside of school. Parents often feel helpless in their efforts to instill proper values in children who are constantly exposed to contrary messages in the media. Public crusades to place stickers on music albums containing violent or sexually explicit lyrics and attempts to control radio and television programming illustrate the desire to control the quality of speech to which youths are exposed. Other examples include the FCC's attempted enforcement of a twenty-four-hour ban on indecent radio and television programming and the recent U.S. Senate passage of an amendment of the Child Protection and Obscenity Enforcement Act that regulates the producers of sexually explicit photographs and motion pictures.

Censorship today may thus reflect a feeling that too much useless and destructive speech distracts society from appreciating the more valuable speech. The objections to many forms of advertising provide one such example. Each day, for instance, twelve billion display ads, two and one-half million radio commercials, and over three hundred thousand television commercials are dumped on the public. Advertising consumes approximately 60 percent of all newspaper space, according to industry expert Leo Bogart. During a lifetime, most people will devote a full year and a half to watching commercials.

The presence of so much speech in so many forms, however, can gradually dull the public to the speech that is really important. In an essay entitled "The Decline of Neatness," Norman Cousins speculated that all of the violence in our language has desensitized society to the revulsion or resistance it should feel toward violence.[7] According to Cousins, "youngsters sit transfixed in front of television or motion-picture screens, munching popcorn while human beings are battered or mutilated." Public speech has become so casually violent that society may be becoming desensitized to the problem of violence and brutality in everyday life. Consequently, censorship may seek to reverse the trend of desensitization.

Modern censorship attempts might also reflect a quality-conscious attitude insofar as they seek to eliminate speech seen as a nuisance. With the prevalence of the media, the nuisance role of speech has greatly increased as society has become more noisy. Though a century ago the presence of dissident speech might have been a rarity, today the rarity is silence. Movie theaters now include talking in the prohibited categories that also include smoking. The AMC theater chain states in its advertisements the admonishments: "Silence Is Golden" and "No Talking during Feature." Yet even with this increased sensitivity to the need for silence, movie theaters increasingly find ways to expose their audiences to more types of commercial advertisements.

Such public warnings against talking were not as necessary a generation or two ago. As communal gatherings and experiences have become so few and infrequent, the ones that do occur – such as sharing a movie in a theater – are often polluted with excessive noise. Many people seem to welcome the opportunity to say their piece in front of any group, even if the group is not particularly eager to hear it. Perhaps this also explains the lack of silence in libraries. Like the desire for privacy, there is an increasing desire to watch a movie or read a book without being disturbed.

Another form of speech that is increasingly perceived as an unnecessary nuisance is the protest demonstration. During the 1960s, the antiwar and civil rights demonstrations attracted national attention and their leaders were often exalted as courageous and dedicated activists. Such demonstrations were a unique and fascinating occurrence at that time. Now, almost three decades later, social protest demonstrations seem out of style and disruptive. With greater ability to communicate through the media, the public perceives less need to physically protest. Consequently, its antidemonstration attitude has turned against abortion protesters in their attempt to conduct marches and against advocates for the homeless in their attempts to demonstrate the plight of the homeless.

The campaign against highway billboards also reflects a censorship campaign that is essentially a reaction against nuisance or "too much" speech. Under the 1965 Highway Beautification Act, many highway billboards have been dismantled. Since 1965, more than 700,000 of the 1.1 million signs along the federal interstate and primary highway systems have come down. Antibillboard activists, however, have introduced into Congress an amendment to the act that would allow state and local governments to ban billboards without paying compensation to the billboard owners. These activists often refer to billboards as "visual pollution," "sensory litter" and an "unsightly nuisance." They want to be able to drive their cars over the nation's highways without being annoyed or offended by unsightly speech along the way. And they have resorted to censorship to try to achieve that luxury.

The New York ban on begging in the subways presents yet another example of censoring speech that is considered an unnecessary nuisance. Yet it also reflects a proclivity to avoid controversial or unpleasant speech. Indeed, the perception that society is experiencing an overload of information leads to the desire to weed out the speech that only seems to rile emotions or raise angers. Since so many other controversies face people in their daily lives, they may feel that there is no harm in silencing controversial speech.

The censorship of controversial speech occurs frequently. Politicians and corporate advertisers, just as visiting in-laws, hope to inhibit the expression of anything controversial. The California Court of Appeals recognized this tendency when, in denying the cancelation by a college of a play that dealt with a killing by a black policeman of a white suspect, it declared that college officials "were merely concerned with avoiding the discomfort and unpleasantness" the play might cause.[8] In another incident, a South Bend, Indiana, group sought to convince a cable television provider to cancel a controversial program entitled "Race and Reason," which was sponsored by a group called the White Aryan Resistance. The attempt by the Frostburg State University in Frostburg, Maryland, to remove two nude paintings from display during an orientation for prospective students and parents likewise constituted an effort to avoid controversy. And a desire to avoid shocking onlookers prompted the removal of five art exhibits depicting homelessness from storefront windows in Portland, Maine.[9]

The public reaction against too much speech carries over to the desire to censor advertising that is considered both unnecessary and destructive. Advertising of alcohol, tobacco, and gambling services often comes under fire as being needless or destructive speech, especially given society's effort to communicate the dangers of smoking, alcohol abuse, and excessive gambling. Furthermore, advertising is also seen as manipulative and consequently dangerous.

Manipulative speech has always fueled opposition. The military handling of the press during the Gulf War, for instance, was not criticized just because the military actively censored and regulated what the media could broadcast and publish. The object of the military censorship was not just national security concerns, but also the manipulation of public opinion. Military leaders used the press to create a certain vision or image of the war that would be politically acceptable to the American public. The public opposition that did occur to this kind of government behavior was based on the desire to eliminate manipulative or inaccurate information from the marketplace of ideas.

The quality-conscious aspect of modern censorship indicates a turning away from quantity considerations. In 1927, Justice Louis Brandeis said that a society's health depends on "more speech, not enforced silence." Today, the feeling is that society has enough speech and information. Continually beset with new technologies that produce more and more information and speech, the public increasingly wants to stop the unmanageable flow of new ideas and to process the existing information and speech. With more information and more voices entering the marketplace through the media, society seems increasingly prone to narrow that marketplace.

Censorship attempts in the early twentieth century took a different approach to the quantity of information in the marketplace. Trying to maintain a more traditional society, censorship advocates sought to exclude certain radical and dissident speech. This censorship campaign focused on the content of the speech and related to certain underlying social and political problems. It rested on a belief in, and fear of, the power of such speech.

Today, however, censorship often attempts to ferret out speech that lacks any meaningful substance or content. It is an effort to purify the marketplace of ideas and to eliminate the less meaningful or irrelevant information. Similarly, the contemporary opposition to pornography differs from the era of the 1920s in that it no longer seeks primarily to censor all expressions of sex – just the abusive and violent images of sex. The difference is also revealed in the specific object of the censors: D. H. Lawrence in the 1920s, and *Hustler* magazine in the 1980s.

Contemporary censorship further reflects a reaction against the perceived bad quality of mass media, just like the bad quality of fast food. In the 1990s, where the emphasis increasingly appears to be on quality and competitiveness, censorship campaigns are often an attempt to improve the quality of American speech.

8

Censorship and the Breakdown of Community

Individual rights in a democratic society have always presented something of a problem. Though free societies have been described as protecting both democratic freedoms and individual liberties, an inherent tension exists between these two kinds of freedom. Too much democracy may mean too little liberty, and too much individual freedom may undermine democracy. There has historically existed a fear that individual liberties and community control are incompatible and even destructive of each other.

Censorship has often reflected this fear. Libertarians who seek expansion of individual freedom see censorship as the effort of an intolerant community to impose conformity and to diminish the range of freedom available to its individual members. Those who believe that too much individual freedom undermines community see censorship as a means of empowering the community to deal with the destructive excesses of individual freedom. Thus, attitudes toward community can influence opinions concerning censorship.

According to the traditional libertarian analysis, censorship often results from too much community. These libertarians tend to link community with censorship. Too much of the former will lead to the imposition of the latter. Consequently, libertarians not only oppose censorship, but they are also inclined to resist the strengthening of community because of their belief that such strengthening will inevitably lead to a curtailment of individual freedoms.

This perceived tension between freedom and community reflects a long-standing view within American liberal political thought. The drafters of the First Amendment intended it as a necessary protection from the encroaching power of the majority upon the individual. According to American political ideology, the majority could not be trusted to protect the rights of the individual. From this ideology of conflict between democracy and liberty came a libertarian fear of the power of the community to censor. As censorship campaigns arose in local communities, opponents saw the community as antagonistic to speech freedoms and intolerant of diverse expressions. They came to believe that the way to prevent censorship was to build up protections against the community. Consequently, the First Amendment became a weapon against, and an adversary to, the community.

This libertarian antagonism to community has generally prevailed throughout this century. Free speech scholars have associated the occurrence of censorship with an active and strong community: the stronger the community, the stronger the push for censorship. When censorship has occurred, the libertarian remedy has often been to find ways to check or diminish the power of the community. However, this remedy may in fact be the wrong response, because the libertarian view of community and censorship may be an incorrect view.

Censorship occurs more often not in strong communities but in weakened, instable, and anxious communities. Communities that feel threatened by dislocating changes and that have lost some of their communal bonds are more prone to express their sense of anxiety through censorship. It seems logical that healthy, secure communities will not respond as harshly toward dissident speech as will communities with greater insecurities. For the latter, censorship may be an attempt, albeit negative, to achieve some communal unity and values. Indeed, the worst manifestations of the censorship impulse, like those found in the hateful intolerance of the Ku Klux Klan, have seemed to emanate from the weakest, unhealthiest, and least progressive communities.

The history of censorship in America demonstrates a relationship between community anxiety and censorship campaigns. One of the first censorship crusades in America occurred in a community intensely insecure with its identity and future. The witchcraft trials in Salem in the seventeenth century were an attempt by the Puritan leadership to reinvigorate and redefine their community, which was undergoing secularizing changes with the increased immigration and the declining social control and homogeneity in the colony.[1] In a community fraught with insecurity and anxiety over the future of its puritanical theocracy, the impulse to censor dissident speech became stronger and resulted in the most severe type of censorship: death by execution. By branding social dissenters as witches, the Salem leaders sought to censor speech that challenged traditional Puritan beliefs.

Many later censorship campaigns in America occurred in communities uncertain and anxious about the changes that had been thrust upon them. The nineteenth-century vice-society movement provides one such example. This movement was a response to the deep-seated fears in the post–Civil War years about the future of urban communities in the United States.[2] It arose from the dislocating changes forced upon urban communities by rapid industrialization and immigration. Consequently, this censorship movement aimed at providing a sense of unity and moral identity to communities that were seemingly breaking apart. With cities increasingly infested with the social problems of crime, overcrowded housing, unemployed immigrants, and children not being properly educated, censorship was an effort to at least rid the city of immoral speech. This effort fit in with the later progressive goal of ridding the cities of social evils, improving social hygiene, and providing for child welfare. Yet the history of American progressivism shows that the more the actual social problems were addressed, the less frequent were the attempts to curtail speech and engage in censorship.[3]

The book censorship crusade in the 1920s similarly reflected a search for moral and social rejuvenation. During this anxious decade preceding the Great Depression, in which the United States had received another great wave of immigrants from war-torn Europe, many communities were undergoing tremendous pressures. The Bolshevik Revolution in Russia and the influence of the Jazz Age brought changes and anxieties to communities about the survival of the American way of life. Communities were caught in a tug-of-war between the modern and the traditional. This was the decade of the Scopes trial, in which the modern secular America clashed with the traditional fundamentalist America. The book censorship movement was an effort by traditionalists to make the community safe for virtue and morality. Campaigns against obscene literature, such as the novels of D. H. Lawrence, were part of an effort to return the community to an idyllic model of the past. Likewise, with the breakdown of old taboos during the Jazz Age, the censorship movement was an attempt to reassert social control.

The Red raids and the book seizures of the 1920s evidenced this communal anxiety. Opponents of the literature of the 1920s expressed preference for the "old masters of fiction" and feared that the new literature "indicated a national obliteration of the moral sense."[4] The formation of the Clean Books League also reflected a longing for a return to an era in the past when everyone respected the law and attended church. Thus, censorship was a response to social changes that caused an identity crisis for the community.

As communities were forced to actively address social changes in the

1930s, however, censorship waned. The image of censorship turned more negative in comparison to the activist and positive images of social reform and child welfare. Because of the social action of the 1930s, the decade was relatively free of censorship. Communities were actively and urgently engaged in community work – censorship seemed too trivial an endeavor. The book censorship movement of the previous decade was now seen as a diversionary activity of a country that had no clear social vision or national purpose. Furthermore, the sight of the Nazi book-burnings in Germany in the 1930s aroused in Americans the desire to create communities of greater tolerance and freedom.

The censorship pattern of the first half of the twentieth century reveals that more troubled communities are more likely to censor. For instance, the early 1920s were a time of much censorship activity in New York City. Unsurprisingly, New York was a very turbulent and heterogeneous community at the time. The far more unified and homogeneous community of Boston, on the other hand, experienced less censorship during this period. However, as Boston social life became more tense and conflicted in the late 1920s, the city experienced a corresponding increase in censorship.

When communities undergo changes that cause their members to feel a loosening or disappearance of their social bonds, they react particularly harshly to disturbing or divisive speech. Such speech becomes a symbol for what is wrong with the community. The weaker the actual ties of community, the more influential are the symbolic ties provided by speech. Through an enforced harmony of public expression, the insecure community tries to keep alive the illusion that it is strong and unified. Individuals likewise seek to maintain the facade that they are all bound together in a community from which they derive their social identity. Thus, censorship is used to control the appearance of the community and to mask the unsettling reality.

This relation between community and censorship has particular relevance today, as the breakdown of communities has been widely acknowledged. Individuals have far less community involvement than they did generations ago. Many of the community building blocks, including the family, volunteer associations, and state and local politics, have been weakened in modern society. The alarming state of political apathy reflects and parallels the decline in communal involvement.

Although freed from the tyranny of small-town traditional values and roles, Americans have not found a sufficient communal substitute for the present age. Consequently, and as the pollsters proclaim, there is a widespread feeling of powerlessness and victimization in today's impersonal community, and psychologists often cite the emptiness felt by individuals in the communally void world of the 1990s. Indeed, communal bonds have greatly eroded since Alexis de Tocqueville observed

Americans' enthusiasm and proclivity for joining together in communities and voluntary associations.

The reality of community in contemporary America has suffered, and censorship campaigns often reflect the social anxiety over this reality. In addition, however, sociologists speculate that the very nature of our public language influences the formation of community. In *Habits of the Heart*,[5] the authors argue that community has suffered because Americans lack a language to express communal values and ideals. According to the authors, the majority of Americans have no language with which to articulate their reasons for communal commitments that transcend the individual, and without a moral language that goes beyond the self, individuals cannot live a truly communal life. Thus, with this connection between speech and community, it is reasonable that Americans would try to create community by negative means – such as censoring speech unsupportive of community – if they cannot do so by positive means – by creating a language of community or building the reality of community.

The highly visible role of speech in a media society renders it vulnerable to censorship by a community seeking to remedy its insecurity and anxiety. The temptation, of course, is to think that the problem will go away if the signs of the problem go away. And in a highly developed media society, speech expressing communal insecurity receives widespread and indiscriminate publication. It becomes the most blatant sign of communal breakdown. Indeed, the television image of a decrepit slum carries more influence than the reality of that slum itself. Furthermore, the expression of that problem can be more easily and quickly censored than the actual problem of urban housing can be addressed or remedied.

Strong, healthy communities, on the other hand, are less susceptible to censorship movements based on communal insecurity. Such communities tend to have clear self-identities and are secure in their communal bonds and outlook for the future. They do not see speech, even dissident and disturbing speech, as a threat, because they do not generally feel threatened or imperiled.

At the foundation of communities lies the family. The strength or insecurity of the family in turn influences the strength of the general community. And at the center of the concerns of family and community stands the child. Child welfare, therefore, greatly determines the stability of both family and community. Unsurprisingly, in communities in which child welfare is in a troubled state, censorship frequently occurs on matters that closely involve children and child development.

The prevalence of television and the decreasing parental supervision of children's television viewing habits have resulted in a growing concern for the impact of television programming on children. This concern accompanies more general concerns for child welfare in communities that have become less hospitable to children. The dangers of child abuse, drug addiction, urban crime, and declining educational opportunities all threaten the health and development of children in modern society. Given this community breakdown on child welfare, censorship activity toward speech perceived as negatively influencing children has increased. For instance, communities have banned the sale of certain types of music, as well as trading cards depicting criminals, to children.[6] As discussed previously, parent and community groups successfully convinced the FCC to adopt rules that would create a twenty-four-hour ban on indecent radio and television programming.[7] According to the Children's Legal Foundation, a group supporting the ban, such a rule was necessary to protect the viewing children from indecent programming.[8] The various movements to censor advertising aimed at children, such as junk-food advertising, also reflect a communal anxiety over the loss of control of child development. This anxiety results from the parental inability to monitor the impact of media upon children, but may also reflect a tendency to shift some of the responsibility for child welfare from parents to the media.

Educational censorship further indicates a communal anxiety over child welfare.[9] During the 1980s and continuing into the 1990s, censorship occurred increasingly in America's schools. According to the *Newsletter for Intellectual Freedom*, schools continued to ban such books as *The Adventures of Tom Sawyer, The Adventures of Huckleberry Finn, The Catcher in the Rye, The Grapes of Wrath*, and *Ulysses*. In a 1982 survey of 860 school librarians, for instance, 34 percent "reported having had a book challenged by a parent or a community that year."[10] Books, films, and other school materials were challenged in one out of three California school districts, according to a survey released December 6, 1990 by the Educational Congress of California. In Warsaw, Indiana, a group of activists campaigned to keep what it considered antifamily values out of schools when it challenged materials used in sex and AIDS education classes. And up until the early 1980s, the Texas Board of Education still prohibited textbooks that mentioned evolution.

This pattern of censorship has continued despite rulings of the Supreme Court in cases like *Epperson v. Arkansas*,[12] in which an Arkansas antievolution law was declared unconstitutional. Despite such judicial warnings, however, attempts to censor textbooks not only continued but actually increased during the 1980s.[13]

These examples reflect only a few of the occurrences of community censorship in the schools during recent years. Such censorship incidents are nothing new. In fact, the period of the 1970s—a time of community insecurity in the wake of the tumultuous 1960s—witnessed many occurrences of school censorship arising from community insecurity. Perhaps the most dramatic incident occurred in 1974 in Kanawha County, West Virginia. During an emotional school book battle, approximately eight thousand students stayed away from school, more than four thousand miners walked off their jobs, picketers closed a number of public facilities, an elementary school was fire-bombed, a person was shot, and another was severely beaten.[14] The cause of this community uproar was a dispute over whether students should be allowed to read certain books to which some citizens objected. Various citizen groups had organized to fight books they felt threatened their basic beliefs and community stability. These textbook opponents felt that most of the language arts texts "contained material that was disrespectful of authority and religion, destructive of social and cultural values, . . . and unpatriotic."[15] The textbooks, which sought to depict the intercultural character of American pluralistic society, were called "un-American" and "ungodly" and were feared to stir up racial troubles. One book opponent even objected to an assignment in a writing book that requested students to discuss how their parents interfered in their private lives. According to the opponent, this assignment forced children to criticize their elders.[16]

The intensity of the Kanawha County conflict prompted the NEA to investigate. In its report, the agency identified one cause of the conflict as the instability and divisiveness of the community. Kanawha County was sharply divided by differences in incomes, lifestyles, religious beliefs, and educational values. The differences between prosperous urban dwellers and poor rural families were particularly sharp, and the NEA found that liberal school administrators had failed to communicate effectively with conservative farmers and miners. Weaknesses in the relations and communications between school administrators and the community had contributed greatly to the censorship conflict.

During the same year, a similar censorship dispute arose in Mississippi. This dispute involved depictions of race relations in various textbooks. Mississippi has been the scene of much racial conflict and violence over the years, and many Mississippi residents felt that the new textbooks, which included discussions of mistreatment of blacks by whites, were too racially oriented and that they did not present "a true picture of the history of Mississippi."[17] Like the incident in Kanawha County, this censorship activity arose from a community insecure and anxious over the changing race relations.

Prior to the 1970s, community insecurities had long contributed to book censorship crusades. Attempts at controlling school books date back to the Civil War. Prior to the war, many Southerners objected to geography books published in the North and that praised New England settlers as role models or that discussed the evils of slavery. During the wave of social tension and cultural change sweeping the nation after World War I, public pressure mounted against supposedly un-American textbooks. The Hearst newspaper chain, for instance, published a series of articles opposing pro-British history books, and the mayor of Chicago, William Thompson, included opposition to pro-British books in his reelection campaign. In 1921, the U.S. commissioner of education banned the teaching of Communism and socialism in the public schools. And, of course, the notorious Scopes trial occurred in 1925, involving the censorship effect of Tennessee's antievolution law.

In the wake of rapid immigration and the rise of Communism and totalitarianism, the American community seemed threatened. Attempting to defend the American way of life, the Advertising Federation of America, the National Association of Manufacturers, and the American Legion waged a monumental campaign against a single textbook series entitled *An Introduction to Problems of American Culture*. The groups charged that the series attacked business, mocked the traditions of American democracy, and made "a subtle plea for abolition of our free enterprise system and the introduction of a new social order based on the principles of collectivism."[18]

The 1950s ushered in another wave of book censorship that rivaled the tide of censorship in the 1920s. Unsurprisingly, both periods of American history have been described as eras of community change and insecurity. In 1953, for instance, a group of individuals asked the Texas State Textbook Commission to ban editions of Geoffrey Chaucer's *Canterbury Tales* and Herman Melville's *Moby Dick* illustrated by Rockwell Kent. According to this group, Kent had Communist connections. During that same year the state legislature of Alabama passed a law that required all textbooks to be accompanied by a statement indicating that the author was not a Communist or socialist. A group called Texans for America opposed history textbooks that "favorably mentioned the income tax, federal aid to farms and schools, the Tennessee Valley Authority, Social Security, unemployment payments, labor unions, racial integration and the United Nations."[19] And in his 1958 book, *Brainwashing in the High Schools*, E. Merrill Root argued that America was losing the Cold War because its textbooks brainwashed students with Communist ideas.

This history of school censorship reflects the anxiety in society over the education and well-being of its children. It also reveals the connections between insecure, anxious communities and the occurrence of censorship. Thus, the censorship activity in the schools today indicates that many communities are feeling especially insecure about the welfare of their children.

Unfortunately, the modern community does not care for children as it once may have. It has become a dangerous place of violence, sex abuse, and drug addiction. Unlike the small-town model that perhaps never totally existed in reality, today's cities prey on the unescorted child. To the wary parent, the streets become havens for potential child kidnappers. This breakdown of community has increased the type of anxiety and paranoia that often lead to censorship campaigns. And this impulse toward censorship has spilled over into areas other than strictly child welfare concerns.

The breakdown of community and its impact on censorship can be seen in certain communities in which blacks and Jews are locked in tense relations. The Crown Heights section of Brooklyn is one such community. In August 1991, an innocent Hasidic Jew was stabbed to death in retaliation for an unrelated traffic accident in which a Jewish driver struck and killed an African-American boy. Since then, there have been demonstrations in which the Israeli flag was burned and other anti-Semitic acts committed by members of the African-American community. Indeed, after the traffic accident in which a black youth was killed, a steady dialogue of anti-Semitism appeared on the black radio station WLIB.

In response to this perceived anti-Semitism, Jews labeled blacks as racist, and the two groups waged a battle to censor the other. For instance, Jews attacked "as a racist pig" an African-American history professor who has criticized and slurred Jews.[20] The attempt to silence or censor that professor reflects their feeling that he was promoting anti-Semitic prejudices. More fundamentally, however, the verbal wars between blacks and Jews and the attempt by each to censor the speech of the other indicate particularly tense and unstable communal bonds between the two groups.

Another example of community anxiety leading to censorship includes an attempt by the Westerly, Rhode Island town council to revoke the entertainment license of a nightclub at which the group 2 Live Crew was to perform. Council members objected to the group's violent and sexually explicit lyrics and called the rap group a threat to public safety, arguing that their appearance would draw a violent element to the beach community. Similarly, the hate crime statutes enacted in many cities across the country indicate attempts to strengthen local community.

The 1991 obscenity trial involving the Mapplethorpe exhibit in Cincinnati and the ensuing congressional debate on funding of the NEA also illustrate the connection between community and censorship. To censorship advocates, Cincinnati seemed the perfect place to conduct an obscenity trial. It had been the home of the Western Society for the Suppression of Vice during the book-banning movement of the progressive era, and the Citizens for Decent Literature was founded there in 1956. In 1991, it seemed to be a strong community of stability and prosperity. As the prosecution discovered, however, Cincinnati was not a community prone to reactionary censorship. A poll conducted shortly before the trial revealed that almost 60 percent of the city residents opposed censorship of the Mapplethorpe exhibit.[21] Moreover, the fear of defense lawyers that suburban jurors coming from close-knit family-oriented communities would be too strongly biased toward censorship also proved unfounded. Despite the judge's denial of the request to exclude such jurors, the jury still acquitted the museum of obscenity charges.[22] Obviously, jurors coming from stronger or more cohesive communities were not as prone to censorship as thought by the defense counsel.

Following the Mapplethorpe exhibit trial, Congress attempted to impose content restrictions on the type of work funded by the National Endowment for the Arts. Various bills were introduced to prohibit NEA funding of indecent or sexually explicit art. A House bill included a provision urging the NEA chairperson to ensure that grants would be awarded after "taking into consideration general standards of decency and respect for the diverse beliefs and values of the American public." There were also rules proposed that would increase the number of lay persons on the NEA's grant-making panel.[23] This struggle over the reauthorization of the NEA, although crystallized in the wake of the Mapplethorpe trial, had actually begun obscurely in 1989 when various religious groups expressed outrage that the photograph by Andres Serrano entitled "Piss Christ" had been included in an exhibition funded by the NEA.

In addition to the question of the type of art that should be publicly funded, the NEA controversy became part of a larger debate on the authority of the democratic community to exercise control over a federal agency that received public funds. Since its founding in 1965, the NEA had grown increasingly distant from the general public, according to critics. The agency had become "a system willfully contemptuous of the public interest and the public voice [and] dedicated to the subsidy of in-group art at the expense of the taxpayers whose money it was so freely spending."[24] Consequently, the art funded by the agency was often not designed for the larger public but for professional colleagues, grant-making panels, and small, well-versed audiences. It was this privileged "system of institutionalized patronage" immune from community control but dependent on community funds that in large part became the object of the forces seeking to more closely regulate the agency.[25]

The campaign against the NEA therefore represented an effort by a democratic community—one that was feeling powerless over that agency and perhaps over the political funding process in general—to retain and exert some political control. Perhaps the public advocated restrictions on the NEA simply because it wanted to bring publicly funded art back to the public and away from the well-organized arts community. Or perhaps it wanted to voice its opinion about the NEA-funded art in the only way it knew – through the political process. Whatever the precise reasons, the NEA controversy revealed an angry and frustrated democratic society.[26]

Censorship activities relating to the democratic community's desire to assert greater control over the use of public funds also occurred in connection with the dispute over regulations regarding the advice doctors can give to patients at publicly funded family planning clinics and the congressional debate over the funding of the Corporation for Public Broadcasting. In a 1991 Supreme Court case addressing the constitutionality of the abortion gag rule, the Court accepted the argument that the government was not censoring anyone but simply dictating how much of money it supplied must be spent.[27] And in legislation passed by the U.S. Senate in June 1992, several restriction were placed on public radio and television stations.[28] Specifically, provisions were made for greater public input into the programming decisions of the Corporation for Public Broadcasting.

The connection between censorship and community insecurity or weakness is one that has not been conclusively proved. To establish a direct tie between community instability and the proclivity toward censorship, more factual research is needed. Yet it seems logical that communities would react just as human beings react. An individual who is defensive or anxious will more likely react harshly to criticism. One who is confident and stable will more readily welcome such speech as an opportunity for debate. If communities react the same way, the traditional understanding of the causes of censorship is inaccurate. The way to avoid censorship battles would then be to strengthen communal bonds. Moreover, the occurrence of censorship may indicate troubles within the community that need to be addressed – troubles other than the presence of disturbing speech.

Community and individual freedom of speech are not as contradictory as envisioned by the traditional libertarian analysis. Indeed, the constitutional protections for speech developed in the twentieth century owe much to the values of democratic community. It was not until judges discovered that free speech was vital for the maintenance of democratic government that the courts began recognizing broad constitutional protections even for extremist speech. A desire to protect democratic community values led to the protection of the individual freedom of speech. Thus, the danger is that an erosion of community life and values may lead to a corresponding weakening of the resolve to protect freedom of speech.

Such a danger exists today. The American community seems caught in a whirlpool of decline and degradation. The media continually describes society's troubles and traumas: the persistence and growth of homelessness, inadequate schools and low-income housing, racial tensions, savage "wilding" attacks by conscienceless youth, a quadrupling of rapes in the last three decades, random shootings of innocent people, a doubling in teen suicides in the last two decades, and an increase of thirty times in the number of 14–17 year olds arrested today from the number arrested in 1950. In desperately searching for the causes and possible remedies for such communal decline, it is easy to focus on the state of American culture and speech – on all of the sex and violence that fills popular culture. In realizing this sad state of public speech, it is not hard to remember the warning that Alexis de Tocqueville gave more than a century ago: Too much individualism might erode community life. Given these recognitions, censorship campaigns against the individual right of free speech might initially seem the appropriate action.

In recent years, a strong sense of community rights has arisen, particularly as a means of empowering communities to address social problems. This notion of community rights has also resulted from the keen sense of anxiety and insecurity over the American community. Indeed, a fear that society is becoming balkanized by competing and conflicting interest groups heightens the need to strengthen and unify communal bonds. As in the past, censorship provides a tempting tool for those seeking to strengthen such bonds, and communal rights provide a tempting justification for the restrictions on freedoms of speech.

The recent campaigns against flag-burning and indecent publicly funded art have been perceived by community advocates not as an assault on speech freedoms but as a crusade to uphold community interests that have appeared lately to come under attack. Thus, to community activists, censorship does not reflect a restriction of individual rights, but is an expression of community rights and standards. When, for instance, Oklahoma City officials refused to grant permits to certain rap groups to perform at public facilities, they denied they were acting as censors and that the issue involved restriction of speech. Instead, they claimed that their action involved only "an issue of community standards."[29] With similar concerns for community interests, some states and communities have resorted to censorship in an attempt to strengthen their local economies. The Colorado legislature, for instance, passed a law punishing any speech that disparages "any perishable agricultural food product." Inspired by an apple scare several years ago that hurt the economic interests of Colorado apple growers, the law was passed to protect the economy from harmful speech. Other communities have tried to suppress speech addressing hazardous conditions created by corporations doing business in those communities for fear that the corporations might leave.

Contributing to communal anxieties and instabilities, which in turn contribute to censorship activity, have been the rapid changes in the media community. The erosion of the prominence and influence of the three television networks, along with the corresponding proliferation of an increasingly fragmented cable media, has signaled a breakdown of the traditional media community that has provided to modern society one of its most powerful common grounds.

During the last several decades, network television became America's mass community and common ground. From the networks came society's news and information, its cultural symbols, its entertainment and education. In a sense, the networks provided the social identity. They furnished perhaps the only common experiences of society and they shaped the public dialogue. They gave an element of commonality—something about which people could speak and relate to each other. In this way, television became America's community.

With the weakening of the networks and the fragmentation and multiplication of the modern media, however, this community has eroded. The proliferation of media outlets, although greatly increasing the amount of speech in society, has nonetheless resulted in another form of community breakdown. The common language of the three networks has been diluted and fragmented among many other competing media forms. Consequently, anxiety results from the uncertainty over the future of society's common bonds and experiences, where in a world of cable there are hundreds of channels instead of just three.

Given this proliferation of speech and the lack of any unifying medium, it is not surprising that many censorship attempts have occurred in connection with the new media. This censorship impulse, however, stems from the same type of communal anxiety that prompted many previous attempts at censorship. With the technological and media changes in modern society, Americans will have to find a new community—perhaps a more personalized community and one rooted in a different kind of commonality or community than provided by the television networks. But as history has shown, this new community can only be found through the free expression of the members of the community, not through the illusion of unity created by censorship.

A Symptom of Insecurity

Psychologists preach that insecurity often leads to fear and defensiveness. For those who are particularly fearful and defensive, not only do sticks and stones break their bones but words most definitely hurt them. It is the insecure and defensive person who most tries to control the things said about or to him. His insecurity, as all who know him realize, becomes a censor on conversation.

As collections of human beings, nations similarly reflect certain human traits. Countries of hard-working individuals, like Japan and Germany, exhibit those traits in their national character. Societies of highly religious individuals, like those in the Middle East, pursue a religious course in their national agenda. In addition, most nations go through personality cycles, as do their individual citizens. Countries may have a period of national confidence, followed by one of doubt and insecurity. Naturally, a country pursues a different agenda and follows different goals during those different periods of the national psyche.

The United States has been frequently characterized as a nation of unbounded optimism and self-confidence. Under this characterization, many foreigners must think that Americans never feel fear or self-doubt or insecurity. But of course, they do — the proliferation of psychological self-help books attests to the prevalence of those feelings. And American history attests to the periodic recurrence of insecurity in the national psyche. Symptoms of these bouts of insecurity have usually included increased censorship activity in society. Censorship often occurs, according to columnist Nat Hentoff who frequently writes about First Amendment issues, "when the nation is most fearful: a time of war, for instance, or during a period when there is much anxiety about an outside menace."[1] Therefore, understanding social motivations toward censorship may require an understanding of American insecurity.

Periods of insecurity have strangely alternated with times of strong national confidence and purpose. During times when any nation should have felt fearful and insecure, America has instead exhibited a determined self-confidence. For instance, during the trauma of the Great Depression and the dangers of the two world wars, America has displayed an optimistic confidence about the future. Yet after victory was achieved in each of those wars, the country slipped into a period of nagging doubts and fears about its social fabric and national security. The post–World War II era came to be known, in W. H. Auden's phrase, as the age of anxiety.

This alternation between confidence and insecurity dates back to the unique circumstances of America's birth. It became a nation separated from the dangers of a warring Europe by a vast ocean. This geographical fact, along with the plenitude of natural resources, gave a strong sense of security to the new nation, as did the fact that most settlers in the new land were neither paupers nor princes. This middle-class aspect of society provided additional stability and homogeneity. On the other hand, the immigrant nature of American society caused, and has continued to cause throughout history, social tensions and anxieties about the national identity and culture. No cultural glue was provided by common ethnic identities, ancient historical traditions, or religious affiliations. Consequently, American history has been a constant and anxious searching for national identity.

Also contributing to the country's nagging sense of insecurity were the high expectations it had set, and continues to set, for itself. From the Puritan's mission to establish in the New World a "city on a hill," to Woodrow Wilson's grand expectation that the country single-handedly could bring peace and democracy to the world, to contemporary Americans who fear that this nation is no longer number one in the world, the United States is expected by its citizens to be the best and the brightest and the strongest and the most morally virtuous nation on earth. However, this belief in the unique and special destiny of the United States also causes much insecurity when that destiny seems threatened.

The national bouts of insecurity have often involved fears associated with four primary concerns: national survival, the future of American democracy, economic success, and social identity and unity. The first fear has often been the most intense. Despite their relative geographic isolation from the rest of the world, Americans have nonetheless felt threats to their survival as a community and as a nation. The unexplored, unsettled New World of the seventeenth century posed great dangers to the survival of the settlers. The first colony at Roanoke, for example, completely and mysteriously disappeared during its first winter. The harsh environment, the almost total separation from the kind of civilization the settlers had previously known, the threat of disease and attack by hostile forces, and the uncertainty over how the European nations might interfere in the New World all contributed to a sense of insecurity.

This insecurity over survival led to a movement for independence by colonists who saw England conspiring to take away their liberties and corrupt their political institutions. Yet, following victory in the Revolutionary War, insecurity returned with the War of 1812. During that war, Americans experienced the fear of seeing British troops attack the nation's capitol and burn the White House. Indeed, throughout the nation's formative years, as perceived by many Americans, foreign powers were constantly scheming to control and restrict the course of national development and expansion. The war with Mexico, for instance, reflected the nation's desire to be free of perceived foreign interference.

Notwithstanding America's involvement in two wars with the strongest empire on earth during a period of less than forty years, the greatest threat to the nation's survival probably occurred during the Civil War—a war in which more Americans were killed than in any other war in history. With society being torn apart, the period leading up to and comprising the Civil War years were obviously ones of great insecurity for the still relatively young nation.

Once the Civil War ended and domestic peace returned, America, after a period of rest, became once more caught up in foreign turmoil. With the nations of Europe trying to build and maintain empires that would be closed to American trade, and with a growing sense of insecurity about being left out of this world order, the United States during the 1890s ventured into the dangerous world of empire-building—a venture that ultimately led to the Spanish-American War. A similar fear of national survival dragged the country into the two world wars of the twentieth century. However, even after both wars were over, America felt a heightened sense of national insecurity.

In the 1920s, in the wake of the Bolshevik Revolution in Russia, America feared the influence of Russian immigrants and radical socialists and Communists. It had seen the nations of Europe and Russia fall to totalitarianism and communism. With the failure of Wilson's grand hopes of international prosperity and harmony, Americans felt threatened by the invisible enemy of domestic radicalism. Consequently, the government embarked on a vicious campaign against suspected radicals and dissidents. During the infamous Palmer raids in 1920, for instance, four thousand suspected radicals were arrested in a thirty-three-city dragnet operation conducted on a single night. In supporting these raids, the *Washington Post* answered claims that the First Amendment had been violated by arguing that "there [was] no time to waste on hairsplitting over infringement of liberty."[2]

Similarly, following the failure of victory in World War II to provide a sense of national security, the 1950s witnessed the assault of McCarthyism against suspected Communist sympathizers. The Alger Hiss case prosecuted by Congressman Richard Nixon illustrated the all-consuming fear of Communist infiltration that existed at the time. The escalation of the Cold War and the conflict in Korea further instilled the fear that communism was clawing at America's door. And the arms race convinced many people that with just a push of the button in the Soviet Union – a push that Soviet leaders could not wait to make – the United States would disappear. Indeed, the arms race was propelled by the fear that America was dangerously behind the Soviet Union in its nuclear arsenal. This fear was reflected in Drew Pearson's 1958 book entitled *USA – Second Class Power* and in John Kennedy's campaign rhetoric in 1960 about the missile gap.

National survival insecurities continued throughout the 1960s, 1970s, and 1980s. They were reflected in the U.S. involvements in Southeast Asia, Central America, and the Middle East, which rested on the assumption that communism underlay every conflict around the world and had to be opposed at every single opportunity. The continued arms race, the rise in international terrorism, and the increasing power of the Mideast oil-producing states all contributed to recurring bouts of American insecurity.

The fears and insecurities of Americans over national survival have contributed to the power of certain conspiracy theories in the national psyche. These theories have sometimes involved foreign governments, such as the eighteenth-century belief that the British government was conspiring to take away the liberties of the American colonists and the twentieth-century fear of the conspiring "Red menace" of communism. However, the most gripping of conspiracy theories have focused on the U.S. government itself. One such theory asserts that Franklin Roosevelt secretly dragged the nation into World War II by suppressing warnings of the attack on Pearl Harbor. Another prominent conspiracy theory involves the belief that the government was involved in, or at least has covered up the truth of, the assassination of John F. Kennedy.

Anxieties over national survival have somewhat coincided with periods of insecurity over the future of American democracy. Inspiring the movement for independence in 1776 was the fear that England was conspiring to destroy American democratic freedoms and institutions. Following the war with England, America found itself the only democracy in a world still hostile to such forms of government. Not since ancient Greece had the world experimented with democracy. Consequently, with Europe predicting democracy's demise once again, America was left with no model or guidelines on how to construct and maintain its seemingly fragile political order. Indeed, the system of checks and balances built into the Constitution reflected the framers' own doubts about the feasibility of pure democracy.

Within several years after the ratification of the Constitution, America's insecurities about its democratic form of government received another jolt from the French Revolution. Undertaken in the name of democracy, the French Revolution turned into a reign of terror. Its tyranny and chaos turned the other European nations further against democracy, and the administration of President John Adams feared the disturbing effects of the revolution in the United States. With Jefferson and his Democratic-Republican party competing with Adams's Federalist party for control of the national government, many Federalists feared that, if he came to power, Jefferson's pro-French leanings would bring to America the same kind of terror and chaos occurring in France. Despite this fear, however, Jefferson won the election of 1800 and accomplished the first democratic peaceful transition of political power in the history of the world.

The nineteenth century brought further anxieties to American democracy. The state constitutions imposed restrictions on political participation. Neither women nor blacks nor men without sufficient property could vote. The fear was that if the vote were extended to those people, they would not exercise it wisely and would throw the country into mob rule. Yet demands were being made for wider democratic freedoms.

Andrew Jackson assumed the presidency on a campaign to relax the property restrictions on suffrage. Meanwhile, nineteenth-century feminists were demanding the right to vote, and the abolitionists were demanding an end to slavery. Both of these demands posed threats to the prevailing view of the fragile democracy. These threats and anxieties continued to plague America as the newly freed slaves were given the right to vote and then later deprived of it through various voting restrictions, as women continued to demand the right of suffrage and then finally obtained it in the 1920s. Continual waves of new immigrants arrived in the country and politically challenged the existing leadership, and the civil rights and women's movements of the twentieth century demanded greater political equality.

Insecurities about the future of democracy persist today in the concerns over voter apathy, campaign financing, and an unresponsive political system. Faced with a seemingly intractable incumbency of politicians, several states have passed laws that limit the number terms served by any individual. Worried about the power of interest groups and the corrupting influence of wealthy contributors, many observers feel that the role of the individual in our democracy is eroding. The frustratingly slow pace of campaign finance reform and the reduction of modern political dialogue to media sound-bites has turned off large numbers of the public from participation in politics. And, of course, the decline of political parties leaves many activists worried. Consequently, the public continually hears and reads about the dire straits of American democracy.

In a nation in which the American dream is economic prosperity and generational progress, a third type of insecurity arises when those lofty dreams appear threatened. Ronald Reagan played on those insecurities when he asked voters in his 1980 campaign if they were better off than they were four years ago. Such insecurities are understandable in a nation that for much of its history has had a relatively unregulated economy subject to the winds of the free market. Up until the Great Depression, this uncertain nature of the economy demonstrated itself in the wild, boom-and-bust swings of the business cycles that had produced major economic depressions practically every other decade since the nation's birth.

Free enterprise, like democracy, was a novel idea and a radical experiment when America adopted it as its economic model. Consequently, as with democracy, it was an uncharted and somewhat unpredictable system. Given this uncertainty, any challenges to the prevailing capitalist ideology were perceived by the public as a threat to the fragile and experimental American way of life.

The two primary challenges that exposed the nation's economic insecurities were the union movement and the various reform periods that attempted to impose government regulation on the economy. In response to the union organizing campaigns throughout the late nineteenth and early twentieth centuries, corporations reacted with the same harsh and violent vengeance that would be used against an attacking aggressor. The public generally acquiesced in this brutal reaction because of its fears about the health of the economic system. These same fears and insecurities continued to surface throughout the union movements and labor strikes of the twentieth century. Such insecurities are illustrated in a remark made in 1946 by Charles Wilson, president of General Electric: "The problems of the United States can be captiously summed up in two words: Russia abroad and labor at home."[3] Just as Russia threatened America with missiles, unions threatened economic health and social stability.

Like unionism, attempts to regulate the economy have raised public fears and insecurities, even when those regulations have promised to benefit the majority of Americans. The regulatory reforms inspired by the populist and progressive movements, as with the regulatory scheme enacted through the New Deal, all met with the same criticism: They would undermine the economy and lead inevitably to socialism or collectivism. Each business regulation, from child labor rules to workplace safety requirements to the Securities and Exchange Commission supervision of the stock market following the Great Crash of 1929, to implementation of the social security and workers' compensation systems, was predicted to destroy the American economic system.

Similarly, in response to the economic regulation implemented during the 1960s and 1970s, business interests claimed that such regulations would contaminate and suffocate the economy. The Reagan administration also played on this fear when it moved to deregulate various industries and to significantly cut taxes. Interestingly, the public supported this tax cut, which was aimed primarily at the relatively small numbers of wealthy taxpayers, largely because of its insecurity over the health of the economy in general.

Economic insecurities currently reveal themselves in the public anxiety over America's trade deficit with Japan. A plethora of books published in the last several years argue that America has become a second-class power and that it is hostage to the Japanese economic might. The public discussions accompanying Paul Kennedy's 1987 book, *The Rise and Fall of the Great Powers*, revealed that Americans fear not only economic decline but any change that keeps the United States from being the number one economic power in the world. Indeed, the recent fears of Japanese dominance mirror the anxieties raised by the Arab states during the oil embargoes of the 1970s.

The current economic insecurity, however, is not confined to national fears of foreign competitors – it is also nagging the personal expectations of individuals across the country. With economic growth sluggish, with homes becoming increasingly more difficult to buy, and with many traditional middle-class jobs disappearing, many Americans fear that economic life will not be better for future generations. Barbara Ehrenreich outlined this national anxiety in her recent book, *Fear of Falling: The Inner Life of the Middle Class*.

The fourth insecurity that has historically plagued America is the anxiety over America's national and cultural identity. This insecurity seems particularly intense at the present time. It arises from the racial, ethnic, and religious diversity of American society. Yet social tensions and cultural conflicts are not recent occurrences. They developed long ago with the first influx of diverse immigrant groups, and with these social tensions came cultural insecurities.

The antiimmigrant crusades of the nineteenth and early twentieth centuries stemmed from the fear that America was threatened by powerful, sinister, and conspiratorial adversaries. This fear was based on a fear of such supposedly un-American peoples as Catholics, Jews, and Slavs. With the rapidly changing demographic make-up of the nation, insecurities arose regarding the cultural identity and unity of America – and consequently these fears translated into an attempt to define Americanism according to the ethnic and religious identities of the people already here.

Later in the twentieth century, this same fear translated into a reaction against such un-American ideas as socialism and secular humanism. Like the previous reaction against peoples perceived to be un-American, this more recent movement shared the belief that America is a fragile paradise susceptible to destruction from within. The insecurity over a definition of Americanism continues to show itself in the nation's gender and racial tensions and in the debates over multiculturalism.

Anxieties over social unity have also resulted from the perceived fragmenting of American society. As the country increasingly recognizes the uniqueness of its many ethnic and racial groups, the fear is that society will fragment into a collection of competing groups. The controversy over bilingualism expresses this fear. Moreover, anxieties over social unity reflect the fear that conflict and differences are inherently unnatural and unresolvable.[4] American mythology sees disharmony and conflict as abnormal and as the result of some evil force that threatens to sabotage the American dream. Thus, instead of accepting the diversity of American society and the inevitable conflict among different groups of people, this insecurity interprets it as an assault on Americanism.

The anxiety over cultural identity also occurs with respect to the recurrent debate on traditional values. Such debates have often ignited public anxieties during periods of increased immigration, when peoples of differing backgrounds and cultural values have crowded into America's cities. Indeed, Prohibition was an outgrowth of the fear of the supposedly immoral and socially unfit, alcohol-guzzling immigrants of the early twentieth century. The insecurity over American values has continued in recent decades, as revealed by the activities of the Moral Majority and the increased politicization of moral issues such as abortion. Intense emotional battles on such issues as affirmative action, gay rights, secular humanism, school prayer, and family values further demonstrate America's insecurity about cultural identity in a diverse and multicultural society.

These cultural insecurities, along with the other American insecurities about national and democratic survival and about economic progress and momentum, have frequently coincided with increased censorship activity. Particularly strong has been the relationship between anxieties over national and political survival and the occurrence of crusades to censor supposedly dangerous and subversive ideas. Indeed, the first national campaign of censorship occurred during one such period of anxiety and just seven years after the First Amendment was ratified. This censorship campaign was highlighted by the passage of the Alien and Sedition Act of 1798.

America in 1798 was caught in the middle of a war between England and postrevolutionary France. Fearing an Anglo-American alliance, the French began seizing American ships trading with England. Meanwhile, America had been experiencing a steady influx of immigrants uprooted by the French Revolution. This growing number of aliens alarmed the ruling Federalist party of John Adams. The Federalists suspected that the influx had brought a multitude of Jacobin sympathizers – revolutionaries from France who were allegedly spreading the reign of terror from nation to nation. The French Revolution, which had begun in 1789, had by 1794 become a bloodbath that even its instigators could not escape. The fear among the Federalists was that similar revolutions would engulf America.

This fear and insecurity also made the Federalists think that the Democratic-Republican party of Jefferson served as a front for the Jacobins. The Federalists realized that the new immigrants almost unanimously supported Jefferson's party and that Jefferson himself was sympathetic to the French Revolution, seeing it in its less extreme forms as an outgrowth of enlightened democratic thought. Thus, not only did the Federalists fear war with France, but they also feared that they would be removed from government by the conspiring Jeffersonians. This insecurity flourished in the climate of xenophobic war hysteria. The paranoid Federalists especially feared criticism in the press and closely monitored unfriendly newspapers. Suspecting that French armies were preparing to invade the United States and that the criticism levied by the Jeffersonians against the government would pave the way for the foreign invaders, the Federalists enacted the Alien and Sedition Act. This act imposed broad censorship on political expression by prohibiting criticism of the government.

When the insecurity over a war with France ended, and when Jefferson won the presidency in 1800, government censorship activity greatly diminished. It reappeared, however, as the country plunged into the Civil War. In fact, military censorship of the news media originated during the Civil War and continued to occur during every subsequent military conflict in which the United States became involved. Moreover, during the Civil War, both the North and the South tried to censor the speech of dissidents, who the respective governments feared

would cause social unrest and interfere with the war efforts. Yet as the
South occupied a more insecure and vulnerable position throughout the
conflict, Southern censorship was more harsh than was Northern censorship.

Anxiety over national security again led to censorship of political
speech during World War I. As in 1798, the influx of new immigrants
and the fears of foreign infiltration, combined with the breakout of war
in Europe and the Communist revolution in Russia, created a state of
fear that resulted in passage of the Espionage and Sedition Acts. These
acts, like the Alien and Sedition Act of 1798, punished criticism of the
government's war effort. The paranoia of the age had caused even a
freedom-loving leader like Woodrow Wilson to turn against free speech.
This censorship continued after the war, with further prosecutions
under the act and with the "Red raids" against suspected radicals and
dissidents. The fear of Soviet communism had begun, and would continue to inspire censorship activities throughout most of the twentieth
century.

The fears caused by the war and the Soviet revolution spilled over
into insecurities about the purity of American society. A desire to elevate or rejuvenate society, so as to strengthen it against foreign corruption, inspired the purity campaigns of the 1920s aimed at censoring
immoral literature. This censorship activity also aimed at maintaining
social control by upholding the old social taboos through censorship.

Similar to the experience of the first world war, America underwent
another period of insecurity and censorship in the wake of World War
II. As the Cold War broke out in the 1950s, Americans found themselves gripped by anxiety over their national security. Political censorship focused on such un-American ideas as socialism and communism.
Once again, the fear of communism and foreign infiltration lay at the
root of the censorship movement.

After the end of the second world war, efforts to stem the spread of
communism became a dominant part of U.S. foreign policy. The Truman Doctrine, the Marshall Plan, the Berlin Airlift of 1948, the North
Atlantic Treaty of 1949, and the Mutual Security Act of 1951 were all
attempts to contain communism. However, this policy suffered two severe blows during the second term of the Truman administration. In
1949, China fell to the Communists led by Mao Tse-tung, and in 1950,
North Korean military forces invaded South Korea. Consequently,
many Americans became increasingly anxious over the security of the
free world from Communist aggressors. Compounding these fears were
the 1948 hearings held by the House Un-American Activities Committee relating to the charges by Whittaker Chambers that Alger Hiss, a
top State Department official, had been a Communist.

In this climate of anxiety, there arose an obsession with preventing those with leftist political views from assuming any positions of national prominence or authority. Senator Joseph McCarthy quickly seized upon the perceived threat of Communist infiltration in the federal government and launched a nationwide anticommunist crusade. During the 1952 election, the Republicans campaigned on the triple theme of "communism, corruption, and Korea." McCarthy traveled across the country articulating these fears and anxieties. With the free world marshaled against the threat of Communist infiltration and subjugation, it was not surprising that Americans would be especially sensitive to and fearful of a Communist threat to their own government and society.

As revealed by the experiences following both world wars, America has focused much of its insecurities and fears about national survival on domestic forces and the enemy within. Perhaps this results from the diverse immigrant American population and the fear that not all groups have sufficiently assimilated in the melting pot of society. Even America's fears about an impending war with Japan in 1941 focused on its own Japanese-American population rather than on the external threat posed by the Japanese navy. These insecurities led to the tragic internment of Japanese-Americans in relocation camps. And following the war, American insecurities continued to focus on the fear of domestic subversives and contributed to the notorious and shameful censorship campaign known as McCarthyism

Censorship in the 1950s took many forms. In addition to the laws and government investigations aimed at political dissidents, the movie and television industries received heavy censorship pressures. The Report of Communist Influence in Radio and Television came out in 1950 and prompted an industry blacklisting of suspected radicals. The self-censorship in motion pictures also reflected a paranoia about the presence in Hollywood of a sinister Communist conspiracy set out to destroy the American way of life.

Besides movies and television, books also became the subject of renewed censorship interest in the 1950s. The Gathings Committee, for instance, was established to propose legislation that would have created a federal censorship board. Operating under the belief that cheap paperback books had become a serious moral threat to the country, the committee concluded that pornography might well be a Communist plot.[5] Even *The Grapes of Wrath* was attacked on the belief that John Steinbeck was a Communist.[6]

After the end of McCarthyism, the next period of national insecurity occurred in the 1960s during the military escalation in Vietnam. The fear of the domino effect of international communism had contributed to U.S. involvement in Vietnam. And the fear of Communist infiltration in American society once again returned with the claims that the social protests and civil rights demonstrations were instigated by Communist agents. In 1968, Richard Nixon played to this fear with his law and order platform. Curiously, given all of the social and international crises, one of the strongest planks of this platform involved the censorship of pornography.

Though the United States retreated from extensive military entanglements after Vietnam, the aggressive anti-Communist foreign policy of the Reagan administration revived the old national insecurities. The arms build-up and the proposed Star Wars defense system brought back the fears of nuclear confrontation with the Soviet Union. These fears and paranoias, as before, fed the censorship impulse. This impulse, for instance, reacted against the 1986 ABC miniseries "Amerika," which portrayed a Soviet occupation of the United States. Curiously, much of the censorship pressure came from liberal critics: Ted Sorenson threatened to sue ABC for its negative depiction of the United Nations.

In connection with its escalation of the arms race and its increasing military involvements in Lebanon, Grenada, and Central America, the Reagan administration embarked on a campaign to deny national security information to the press, which it often considered to be dupes of the Soviet Union. In 1982, for instance, President Reagan signed an executive order that greatly increased the classification of government documents. As Reagan explained in a memorandum, such measures were necessary to counteract the "left-of-center working press which put its prejudices above its responsibilities to the public."[7]

This insecurity and paranoia toward the press curiously came from an administration that appeared to be very successful at communicating through the media. It caused the government to continually censor the press by depriving it of information to which it previously had access. During the invasion of Grenada in October of 1983, for instance, the government excluded reporters from covering the initial landing. In 1984, Reagan expanded the categories of documents exempted from the Freedom of Information Act. Two years later, the White House adopted thirteen measures to increase information security, including the prosecution of officials for leaks of information to the press. A November 1986 memorandum from the national security advisor further limited release of government information and restricted access to security data by creating a new "sensitive" category. The government also announced that bureaucrats with access to classified information had to take lie detector tests during investigations of certain information leaks to the press. The administration even placed greater controls on scientific information and communication, particularly in connection with the access of foreign scientists to such information.

By escalating tensions with the Soviet Union and engaging in military actions around the world, the Reagan administration heightened

American insecurities. Not surprisingly, greater censorship activity accompanied this escalation. This pattern was again repeated during the Gulf War in 1991. The censorship controls placed on the press by the government have been well reported.[8] Because of the insecurities felt during times of military conflict, the public by an overwhelming margin supported such censorship measures.[9] So strong were public insecurities that frequent acts of violence against antiwar protesters were reported. College basketball fans even booed and jeered Seton Hall University's Marco Lokar, an Italian citizen, who refused to wear an American flag on his uniform.

Thus, censorship has often arisen in the United States during times of insecurities about the survival of the nation and of its democratic system. So too, however, has it arisen during periods of insecurity about America's cultural identity and social unity.

As a pluralistic, immigrant nation with no inherited cultural identity, America quite naturally has experienced periodic insecurity regarding its identity and cultural values. Moreover, the belief in the United States as a unique and virtuous democratic society born out of the melting pot of the world's immigrants further intensifies the nation's insecurities, especially during periods of racial tensions and social unrest. These insecurities, when aggravated, have in turn led to various censorship movements relating to cultural issues. As the censorship drives have demonstrated, Americans believe in a close relationship between speech and the social fabric, especially in the modern media age.

The history of cultural censorship stretches back to colonial times. As colonial society began to change because of immigration, and as the social leaders felt a loss of control, censorship of ideas posing a challenge to the existing social order ensued. The Puritans' censorship of suspected witchcraft was one such example. Following the nation's birth, cultural tensions continued to pull at the social fabric. In addition to immigrant pressures, the tensions between North and South produced much cultural anxiety. Given the great differences between the two cultures, the question was which one would control the national identity. Naturally, censorship resulted, particularly in the school textbooks. Southerners would not use books that unfavorably depicted the South nor ones that exalted the Yankee way of life.

The social strife in the late nineteenth century caused by the emerging union movement also created much cultural conflict. Contradicting the cultural belief that America was a classless society and that capitalism fostered social harmony, the working-class movement caused alarming insecurities about the health and future of society. Consequently, public pressure arose to censor the union organizers and socialist advocates.

The immigration of the early twentieth century brought more cultural insecurity in the 1920s. In addition, certain technological and demographic changes were producing social anxiety. The mobility created by the automobile, the increased attention to entertainment in the Jazz Age, the modernizing influences of new technology, and the movements of population from rural to urban areas all changed the character and identity of American society. Traditionalists reacted to these changes with censorship. Censored subjects in books and movies included profanity, illegal traffic in drugs, white slavery, sex hygiene, venereal disease, ridicule of clergy, desecration of the flag, techniques for committing any crime, sympathy for criminals, men and women in bed together, and prostitution.[10]

The tensions between modernism and fundamentalism resulted in the censorship of the concept of evolution, as revealed in the Scopes trial. Fearing an increasingly secular and irreligious society during the Roaring Twenties, groups including the Catholic church became heavily involved in censorship, particularly of sexual matters. The increasing involvement of women in the public arena threatened traditional sex and family roles and further heightened the pressures for censorship of sex. Such censorship also responded to the anxiety that the traditional values of American democracy might be declining.

In addition to the challenges to religious and family values, the ethnic makeup of America in the 1920s was undergoing great change. The social insecurities caused by rapid immigration in turn bred censorship attempts aimed at the new ethnic groups and at upholding a vague sense of Americanism. Coinciding with the government censorship of radical immigrants, private groups like the American Legion, the Ku Klux Klan, the Daughters of the American Revolution, and the Knights of Columbus also pushed for censorship of what they considered to be un-American people and ideas. Book censorship was a common endeavor, and these groups sought to ban books that failed to promote patriotism or that seemed to advocate such un-American ideas as socialism.

The creed of Americanism became a symbol of cultural identity. It also became a substitute for other more tangible signs of American culture and society. It developed during a period of much social instability. Thus, any speech that criticized or contradicted the creed of Americanism raised anxieties and was labeled un-American. The censorship of such un-American speech prevailed during the anxious era of the 1920s and resurfaced during a similar period after the second world war.

The censorship of un-Americanism in the 1950s was particularly focused on the television and motion picture industries, since they were perceived as having a profound influence on shaping the cultural identity. Furthermore, cultural insecurities heightened as the civil rights and women's movements unfolded throughout the 1950s, 1960s, and

1970s. The traditional consensus and unity of society now gave way to cultural divisions and conflicts. While feminists and civil rights activists wanted to shape society in their interests, conservatives tried to maintain a traditional and unified sense of Americanism. The sexual revolution further intensified the country's insecurities over traditional values. These insecurities coincided with the censorship wave in the 1960s and 1970s pertaining to moral issues.

Within the last several years, cultural insecurity has intensified. The diversity and disunity of society have caused a profound cultural nervousness.[11] Indeed, it seems that the great ideological and political battles of the age are shifting to the terrain of culture. Debates over art, music, television, gender, race, education, and multiculturalism are absorbing the nation's attention and causing the most controversy.

In the cultural civil war that is occurring, both sides are convinced of the moral righteousness of their position and of the sinister intentions of the opposing side. Conservatives, for instance, believe that a radical feminist–civil rights complex seeks to destroy the traditional family, unborn children, and the cultural values of Western civilization. Liberals, on the other hand, perceive intolerant opponents who threaten the progress made on affirmative action, minority rights, and women's freedom to choose an abortion. The emotional intensity of this cultural conflict reflects an underlying cultural insecurity. Expressing such insecurities, some claim that "American culture has been taken over by the enemies of culture."[12] And once again, this insecurity brings censorship.

There have been many recent incidents of cultural censorship attempts. The NEA controversy, the Mapplethorpe exhibit trial, and the obscenity prosecutions of rock groups are just a few examples. Multiculturalism has also caused tensions between those who seek a common cultural identity and those who claim that multiculturalism only fragments and tribalizes society. As with previous social conflicts, such as those involving immigrants, unions, and the civil rights movement, the insecurities brought on by multiculturalism have encouraged censorship. This censorship has occurred in the politically correct movement and in the various speech codes designed to restrict and punish racist and sexist expressions.

Cultural insecurity has also resulted from social conflicts over values. With the traditional family model becoming increasingly rare and with the demands of feminist and gay rights groups becoming increasingly strong, there seems to be little social consensus on cultural values. The insecurity left by this void has pushed religious groups into the political arena to do battle over values. One of the weapons of this battle has been censorship. Abortion, sex, education, popular music lyrics, and television programming have been the subjects of this kind of cultural censorship. The debates over secular humanism and the teaching of creationism have typified the censorship conflicts over cultural values. As late as 1981, the California Assembly passed a bill requiring the adoption of texts that stressed the importance of family, the principles of free market enterprise, respect for the law, and the universal values of right and wrong. Although California's Senate rejected the bill, it reflects the social anxiety over the identity of American society and its cultural values.

Social anxiety has more recently been revealed in the uncertainty over the notion of patriotism. The attempt to define this concept has led to censorship efforts regarding the flag and the Pledge of Allegiance. Like the past efforts to censor un-American speech, the attempt to define patriotism through censorship reflects a deep insecurity about the identity and unity of contemporary society. It is a response to the seemingly irreconcilable cultural conflicts between majoritarians and multiculturalists and between religious values and secular humanism, and it seeks to find cultural unity if only through the enforcement of harmonious expression.

Perhaps cultural issues preoccupy American politics at the present time because the nation is floundering in uncertainty over its economic future. Americans have come to expect and rely upon continual economic growth and dynamism. When that growth stalls, as it has at the present time, insecurity abounds. Because of the budget deficit, the savings and loan crisis, the trade imbalance with Japan, and the nagging recession, the economic future is highly uncertain. Yet because of the relative lack of power of the public to quickly remedy economic problems, this economic uncertainty tends to focus on cultural issues, which leads to the censorship already discussed. However, it also leads to a proclivity to censor speech that increases our economic insecurities. The historic impulse to restrict the picketing of striking workers is one such attempt at censorship. In a more recent example, New York's attempted ban on begging in its subways reflects a censorship of the speech of poverty that all Americans anxiously hope to avoid.

The rise of censorship pressures in contemporary society stems in part from the nervousness pervading nearly every aspect of American life. The size and diversity of the country seem to make it virtually unmanageable. Political and social institutions appear ineffective and fragile. Consensus seems impossible. As a result, collective frustration and insecurity spread. Inevitably, "there is the temptation to turn to simple and direct solutions, to control or ban or limit expression seen as undesirable by whatever means and at every level—school libraries, town meetings, city councils—whenever and wherever values are perceived to be threatened."[13]

Insecurities have long marked the American mindset. As a nation of speech, America has often dealt with its insecurities by reacting against speech. Consequently, during periods when the country is mired in anxiety, censorship more frequently occurs. When the country, on the other hand, has a clearer and more optimistic vision of national purpose, there has often been greater tolerance of diversity and fewer tendencies toward censorship.

Notes

INTRODUCTION

1. "Minister's Suit Asks Ban of Film About Censorship," *New York Times*, May 4, 1992, p. A10.

CHAPTER 1

1. Nicols Fox, "Siege of the First Amendment," *Washington Journalism Review*, December 1990, p. 42.

2. "Influential Book," *New York Times*, November 20, 1991, p. D2.

3. "School Censorship on Rise," *Newsletter on Intellectual Freedom*, November 1990, p. 201.

4. Jon Pereles, "The Best Show? In the Court, Not the Concert Hall," *New York Times*, December 30, 1990, p. E4.

5. Richard Harrington, "Seattle's Ban on Erotic Discs," *Washington Post*, April 1, 1992, p. C7.

6. "Here We Go Again," *USA Today*, April 24, 1992, p. D1.

7. For instance, the national protest against Time Warner Inc., which released the song "Cop Killer" by rapper Ice-T, brought a doubling of the album's sales since the first calls for a boycott of the album. Adding to the notoriety of the protest was a letter signed by sixty members of Congress expressing "[their] deep sense of outrage" over Time Warner's decision to continue distribution of the album whose lyrics were called "despicable" and "vile." Avis

Thomas-Lester and Marylou Tousignant, "Reaction to Ice-T Song Heats Up," *Washington Post,* June 25, 1992, p. C1.

8. "Too Cruel, Live," *New Republic,* July 16, 1990, p. 8.

9. Joe Queenan, "Misfit Metalheads," *Time,* September 30, 1991, p. 82.

10. "Sex Videos Booming Despite Censorship," *Newsletter on Intellectual Freedom* (Office for Intellectual Freedom, American Library Association), September 1990, p. 158.

11. Jonathon Green, *The Encyclopedia of Censorship* (New York: Facts On File, 1990), p. 330.

12. "Excerpts from Bush's Address at University of Michigan," *New York Times,* May 5, 1991, p. A16.

13. See Steve Jones, "Banned in the USA: Popular Music and Censorship," *Journal of Communication Inquiry* 15, no. 1 (Winter 1991): 73–87.

CHAPTER 2

1. *Information Please: Almanac, Atlas & Yearbook: 1991,* 44th Edition (Boston: Houghton Mifflin Co., 1991), p. 376.

2. U.S. Department of Commerce, *Statistical Abstract of the United States, 1990: The National Data Book,* 110th ed., Bureau of the Census, p. 55.

3. Deborah M. Burek, ed. *Encyclopedia of Associations,* 26th ed. (Washington, D.C.: Gale Research, 1992).

4. U.S. Department of Commerce, *Historical Statistics of the United States: Colonial Times to 1970, Part 2,* Bureau of the Census, Series R, 218–223.

5. Ibid., Series R, 93–105.

6. Ibid., Series R, 923.

7. Ibid., Series R, 924.

8. U.S. Department of Commerce, *Statistical Abstract, 1990,* p. 961.

9. See Adam Clymer, "Watergate's Legacy Has Had Mixed Results on Government," *Star Tribune,* June 14, 1992, p. 19A.

10. The report was released October 18, 1990 by Article 19, a London-based organization that seeks to defend freedom of expression. Sheila Rule, "Group Says Press Freedom Is Declining in Britain," *New York Times,* October 19, 1990, p. A7.

11. Lee Burress, *Battle of the Books: Literary Censorship in the Public Schools, 1950–1985* (Metuchen, N.J.: Scarecrow Press, 1989), p. 11.

12. L.B. Woods, *A Decade of Censorship in America (1966–1975)* (Metuchen, N.J.: Scarecrow Press, 1979), p. 82.

13. Ibid., p. 97.

14. Woods, *A Decade of Censorship,* p. 58; Burress, *Battle of the Books,* p. 50.

15. Burress, *Battle of the Books,* p. 27.

16. Eve Pell, *The Big Chill: How the Reagan Administration, Corporate America, and Religious Conservatives are Subverting Free Speech and the Public's Right to Know* (Boston: Beacon Press, 1984), p. 115.

17. A good overall history of movie censorship appears in Gerald Gardner,

The Censorship Papers: Movie Censorship Letters from the Hays Office, 1934 to 1968 (New York: Dodd, Mead, 1987). As Gardner shows, censorship was an integral part of the American movie business for more than a generation. In an effort to prevent government regulation of their industry, filmmakers in the 1930s acceded to self-imposed regulation in the form of the Production Code Administration (PCA).

For a discussion of the government investigation by the House Committee on Un-American Activities of Communists in Hollywood in the 1940s and 1950s, see Bernard F. Dick, *Radical Innocence: A Critical Study of the Hollywood Ten* (Lexington: University of Kentucky Press, 1989).

CHAPTER 3

1. *Miller v. State of California*, 413 U.S. 15 (1973).

2. Edward de Grazia and Roger Newman, *Banned Films: Movies, Censors and the First Amendment* (New York: Bowker, 1982), p. 72.

3. Eve Pell, *The Big Chill: Now the Reagan Administration, Corporate America, and Religious Conservatives are Subverting Free Speech and the Public's Right to Know* (Boston: Beacon Press, 1984), p. 115.

4. Lee Burress, *Battle of the Books: Literary Censorship in the Public Schools, 1950–1985* (Metuchen, N.J.: Scarecrow Press, 1989), p. 52.

5. Michael Kagay, "As Candidates Hunt the Big Issue, Polls Can Give Them A Few Clues," *New York Times*, October 20, 1991, p. B4.

6. George Gallup, Jr., *The Gallup Poll: Public Opinion 1990* (Wilmington, Del.: Scholarly Resources, Inc.), p. 66.

7. Ibid., pp. 74–75.

8. Bill Bryson, *The Mother Tongue* (New York: William Morrow & Co., 1990), p. 100.

9. George Gallup, Jr., *The Gallup Poll: Public Opinion 1989* (Wilmington, Del.: Scholarly Resources, Inc.), p. 24.

10. "Bradley Urges Blunt Talk about U.S. Race Relations," *Minneapolis Star Tribune*, October 20, 1991, p. A4.

CHAPTER 4

1. John Stuart Mill, *On Liberty* (New York: Bobbs-Merrill, 1956), p. 18.

2. The Supreme Court, for example, quoted Mill extensively in *New York Times v. Sullivan*, 376 U.S. 254 (1964).

3. See Archibald Cox, *Freedom of Expression* (Cambridge, Mass.: Harvard University Press, 1981), p. 2.

4. *Journals of the Continental Congress*, 1 (1776): 104, quoted in *Near v. Minnesota*, 283 U.S. 697 (1931).

5. Zachariah Chafee, *Free Speech in the United States* (Cambridge, Mass.: Harvard University Press, 1942), p. 31.

6. Alexander Meiklejohn, *Free Speech and Its Relation to Self-Government* (New York: Harper & Row, 1972), pp. 26–27.

7. 250 U.S. 616, 630 (1919).

8. 274 U.S. 357, 375 (1927) (Brandeis, J., concurring). This view was also restated in *Red Lyon Broadcasting Company v. F.C.C.*, 395 U.S. 367, 390 (1969): "A free flow of information in an uninhibited marketplace of ideas will produce truth."

9. 52 F. Supp. 362, 372 (1943).

10. "After Protests, Sullivan Blocks Teen-Sex Survey," *Minneapolis Star Tribune*, July 20, 1991, p. A6.

11. "No Sex, We're Republicans," *Time*, August 5, 1991, p. 27.

12. C. Everett Koop, *The Memoirs of America's Family Doctor* (New York: Random House, 1991).

13. These regulations were upheld by the Supreme Court in *Rust v. Sullivan*, 111 S. Ct. 1759 (1991).

14. James Dennis, "For the Common Good," *Trial*, September 1990, p. 55.

15. John Taylor, "Are You Politically Correct?" In *1991 First Amendment Law Handbook*, edited by James Swanson (New York: Clark Boardman Callaghan, 1991) p. 78.

16. William A. Henry III, "Upside Down in the Groves of Academe," *Time*, April 1, 1991, p. 66.

17. Ibid.

18. Dinesh D'Souza, *Illiberal Education: The Politics of Race and Sex on Campus* (New York: Free Press, 1991).

19. Constance Hays, "CUNY Barred from Punishing a White Professor," *New York Times*, September 5, 1991, p. B2.

20. Henry, "Upside Down in the Groves of Academe," p. 66.

21. Ibid.

22. Quoted in Roger Kimball, "The Tyranny of Virtue," *Gannett Center Journal* (Spring 1991), p. 155.

23. Ibid.

24. "Taking Offense: Is This the New Enlightenment on Campus or the New McCarthyism?" *Newsweek*, December 24, 1990, p. 51.

25. Dinesh D'Sousa, "In the Name of Academic Freedom, Colleges Should Back Professors Against Students' Demands for Correct Views," *The Chronicle of Higher Education*, April 24, 1991, p. B1.

26. Arlynn Leiber Presser, "The Politically Correct Law School," *ABA Journal*, September 1991, p. 53.

27. Henry, "Upside Down in the Groves of Academe," p. 66.

28. Tony Blass, "Careful What You Say," *Law and Politics*, July 1991, pp. 10–17.

29. D'Souza, "In the Name of Academic Freedom," p. B1.

30. Anthony DePalma, "In Campus Debate on New Orthodoxy, A Counter-offensive," *New York Times*, September 27, 1991, p. A1.

31. Allan Parachini, "Is the Western View the Best?", *Minneapolis Star Tribune*, July 6, 1991, p. A12.

32. Paula Rothenberg, "Critics of Attempts to Democratize the Curriculum Are Waging a Campaign to Misrepresent the Work of Responsible Professors," *The Chronicle of Higher Education*, April 10, 1991, p. B2.

33. Henry, "Upside Down in the Groves of Academe," p. 67.

34. Michel Marriott, "Afrocentrism: Balancing or Skewing History?" *New York Times*, August 11, 1991, p. A1.

35. James W. Carey, "The Academy and Its Discontents," *Gannett Center Journal*, Spring 1991, p. 168.

CHAPTER 5

1. Robert Hughes, "The Fraying of America," *Time*, February 3, 1992, pp. 44–46.

2. These two cultures of the 1920s are described and analyzed by Warren Susman in *Culture as History: The Transformation of American Society in the Twentieth Century* (New York: Pantheon Books, 1984).

3. Nicols Fox, "Siege of the First Amendment," *Washington Journalism Review*, December 1990, p. 42.

4. Paul S. Boyer, *Purity in Print: The Vice-Society Movement and Book Censorship in America* (New York: Charles Scribner's Sons, 1968), p. 57.

5. Ibid., 100.

6. Ibid., 121.

7. Edward de Grazia and Roger Newman, *Banned Films: Movies, Censors and the First Amendment* (New York: Bowker, 1982), p. 92.

8. *Rocky Mountain News*, August 20, 1990.

9. *Edwards v. Aguillard*, 476 U.S. 1103 (1987).

10. Eve Pell, *The Big Chill: How the Reagan Administration, Corporate America, and Religious Conservatives are Subverting Free Speech and the Public's Right to Know* (Boston: Beacon Press, 1984), p. 115.

11. Ibid., p. 111.

12. De Grazia and Newman, *Banned Films*, p. 7.

13. Sidney Blumenthal, "Symbolic Logic," *New Republic*, July 9, 1990, p. 13.

14. Tamar Jacoby, "A Fight for Old Glory," *Newsweek*, July 3, 1989, p. 18.

15. In a commencement speech at Stanford University, for instance, Kirk Varnedoe, the director of painting and sculpture at the Museum of Modern Art in New York, said that "support for the arts is a symbolic battleground on which issues of our national purpose, our collective morality and tolerance, are being contested." *New York Times*, June 15, 1992, p. B5.

CHAPTER 6

1. "Camera Banned, Pens Allowed," *ABA Journal*, August, 1991, p. 16.

2. "2 Live Crew Acquitted," *ABA Journal*, December, 1990, p. 29.

3. Robert Hughes, "The Fraying of America," *Time*, February 3, 1992, p. 47.

4. Frank Kermode, "Whose History is Bunk?" *New York Times Book Review*, February 23, 1992, p. 33.

5. Nicols Fox, "Siege of the First Amendment," *Washington Journalism Review*, December 1990, p. 43.

6. Jerry Taylor, "Bossy States Censor Green Ads," *Wall Street Journal*, August 8, 1991, p. 16.

7. Paul Gustafson, "High Court Will Review St. Paul Hate Crime Law," *Minneapolis Star Tribune*, June 11, 1991, p. A1.

8. "Breaking the Codes," *New Republic*, July 8, 1991, pp. 7–8.

9. *Whitney v. California*, 274 U.S. 357, 374 (1927).

10. This study was conducted by W. L. Marshall of Queens University and reported in the May 1988 issue of *The Journal of Sex Research*.

11. Larry Baron and Murray A. Straus, "Four Theories of Rape: A Macrosociological Analysis," *Social Problems* 34, no. 5 (December 1987): 467–489.

12. Daniel G. Linz, Edward Donnerstein, and Steven Penrod, "Effects of Long-Term Exposure to Violent and Sexually Degrading Depictions of Women," *Journal of Personality and Social Psychology* 55, no. 5 (November 1988): 758–768.

13. The readings in Robert M. Baird and Stuart E. Rosenbaum, eds., *Pornography: Private Right or Public Menace?* (Buffalo, N.Y.: Prometheus Books, 1991) show that there is no consensus regarding the effects of viewing or reading explicit sexual materials. For a recent survey of the scientific evidence confirming that no causal link has been established between pornography and crimes of sexual violence, see Marcia Pally's *Sense & Censorship: The Vanity of Bonfires* (1991), published by Americans for Constitutional Freedom and the Freedom to Read Foundation. In addition, the report of the President's Commission on Obscenity and Pornography (1970) concluded that there was "no reliable evidence . . . that exposure to explicit sexual material plays a significant role in the causation of delinquent or criminal sexual behavior."

14. The Pornography Victims' Compensation Act, now before the Senate Judiciary Committee, is an example of such censorship and, if passed, would allow victims of sex crimes to sue producers and distributors of obscenity if they could prove the crime was somehow incited by the material. In supporting this legislation, feminist author Andrea Dworkin argues that pornographers "make a product that they know dehumanizes, degrades and exploits women; they hurt women to make the pornography, and then consumers use the pornography in assaults both verbal and physical" (Andrea Dworkin, "Pornography and the New Puritans: Letters from Andrea Dworkin and Others," *New York Times Book Review*, May 3, 1992, p. 15). A similar bill has been introduced in the Massachusetts legislature and defines pornography as a violation of women's civil liberties. Both of these legislative proposals have the support of many feminists.

In another case of such censorship, a federal judge in January 1991 ruled that a female welder at Jacksonville Shipyards was harassed by male coworkers who put up graphically sexual posters and calendars. See John Elson, "Passions over Pornography," *Time*, March 30, 1992, p. 52.

15. Free speech advocates, however, oppose such a colored view of censorship. In an essay in the *York Times Book Review* titled "Pornography and the New Puritans" (March 29, 1992, p. 1) author John Irving denounced the Pornography Victims' Compensation bill as a morally reprehensible transfer of re-

sponsibility for any sexual crime away from the actual perpetrator and onto artists and publishers. Some feminists have also opposed the bill as an act of unwarranted censorship. An Ad Hoc Committee of Feminists for Free Expression, whose members include such noted writers as Betty Friedan, Nora Ephron, and Erica Jong, has argued that the Pornography Victims' Compensation Act (S 1521) is a "logical and legal muddle that scapegoats speech as a substitute for action against violence and reinforces the 'porn made me do it' excuse for rapists and batterers." Elson, "Passions over Pornograph," p. 53.

16. Ruth Marcus, "The Bottom Line on Freedom of Speech," *Washington Post National Weekly Edition*, January 14, 1991, p. 33.

17. "Musicland Warned about Rap Album," *Minneapolis Star Tribune*, July 27, 1991.

18. Steve Jones, "Banned in the USA: Popular Music and Censorship," *Journal of Communication Inquiry* 15, no. 1 (Winter 1991): 77.

19. The belief in a causal link between violence depicted in the media and subsequent violent behavior in the audience is not a new conclusion. In 1972, for instance, Surgeon General Jesse Steinfeld stated that "It is clear to me that the causal relationship between televised violence and antisocial behavior is sufficient to warrant appropriate and immediate remedial action."

20. This law was overturned by the U.S. Supreme Court in *Simon & Schuster v. New York Crime Victims Board*, 112 S. Ct. 501 (1991).

21. In a related incident, trials began in June 1992 for dozens of street preachers arrested for disturbing the peace and disrupting business in Beaufort, S.C. *USA Today*, June 8, 1992, p. A3.

22. *Time*, March 5, 1990, pp. 47–51.

23. Recent libel verdicts include a $13.6 million award in September 1990 to auto racing promoters who sued the *Cleveland Plain Dealer* over a report alleging that they had enriched themselves from proceeds of the Budweiser Cleveland Grand Prix; a $28 million award in April 1990 to a heart surgeon who sued KENS-TV in San Antonio over reports alleging that he performed unnecessary surgery on elderly patients; a $2.8 million judgment against the *Pittsburgh Post-Gazette*, which had accused attorney Richard DiSalle of misconduct in drafting the will of a Pennsylvania millionaire; and a $200,000 judgment against the *Hamilton Journal-News*, which came in a suit by an unsuccessful judicial candidate accused of using dirty tricks to promote an investigation of his opponent.

24. *Newsletter on Intellectual Freedom* (Office for Intellectual Freedom, American Library Association), May 1992, p. 87.

25. Randy Furst, "Hundreds Rally against Chops by Braves Fans," *Minneapolis Star Tribune*, October 20, 1991, p. 14A.

26. John Patrick Diggins, "Power, Freedom, and the Failure of Theory," *Harper's Magazine*, January 1992, p. 18.

27. Richard Morin, "When the Name Is Not a Game," *Washington Post National Weekly Edition*, April 29, 1991, p. 36.

28. Don Terry, "Bill to Shield Rape Victims Sparks a Heated Debate in Iowa," *New York Times*, April 26, 1991, p. A16.

29. Paul S. Boyer, *Purity in Print: The Vice-Society Movement and Book Censorship in America* (New York: Charles Scribner's Sons, 1968), p. 57.

30. David Zimmerman, "Lobbying to Pit FCC against NEA," *USA Today*, May 7, 1992, p. D1.

CHAPTER 7

1. *Newsletter on Intellectual Freedom* (Office for Intellectual Freedom, American Library Association), September 1990, p. 162.

2. The Jefferson Center poll was reported in the *Newsletter on Intellectual Freedom*, November 1990, p. 227; the PWA poll was reported in the *Newsletter on Intellectual Freedom*, July 1990, p. 120.

3. *Newsletter on Intellectual Freedom*, March 1992, p. 66.

4. *Newsletter on Intellectual Freedom*, September 1990, p. 161.

5. *Newsletter on Intellectual Freedom*, November 1990, p. 201.

6. *Newsletter on Intellectual Freedom*, May 1990, p. 85.

7. Norman Cousins, "The Decline of Neatness," *Time*, April 2, 1990, p. 78.

8. Reported in "Court Upholds Ruling in Free-Speech Case," *The Chronicle of Higher Education*, August 8, 1990.

9. *Newsletter on Intellectual Freedom*, March 1990, p. 90.

CHAPTER 8

1. Paul Boyers and Stephen Nissenbaum, *Salem Possessed: The Social Origins of Witchcraft* (Cambridge, Mass.: Harvard University Press, 1974). The authors argue that the witch hunt was a quest for community and social identity.

2. Paul S. Boyer, *Purity in Print: The Vice-Society Movement and Book Censorship in America*, (New York: Charles Scribner's Sons, 1968).

3. Ibid., p. 43.

4. Ibid., p. 100.

5. Robert N. Bellah, Richard Madsen, William M. Sullivan, Ann Swidler, and Steven M. Tipton, *Habits of the Heart: Individualism and Commitment in American Life* (Berkeley: University of California Press, 1985).

6. The Louisiana legislature passed a bill to outlaw the sale of certain music to minors ("Lifeline," *USA Today*, June 19, 1992, p. B2) and, leading a national wave of protest, Nassau County, New York passed a measure banning the sale of trading cards depicting criminals to children under seventeen (Wayne King, "Republicans Seek to Sell New Jersey Nonprofit TV," *New York Times*, June 16, 1992, p. B4).

7. This ban was declared unconstitutional by the United States Court of Appeals for the District of Columbia on May 17, 1991. (*Action for Children's Television v. FCC*, 932 F.2d 1504 (D.C. Cir., 1991)).

8. Edmund Andrews, "Ban on Indecent Programs Rejected," *New York Times*, May 18, 1991, p. B10.

9. Examples of such censorship are found in attempts by schools to censor the expressions of students. Although the 1988 *Hazelwood* ruling condones some kinds of censorship, there has been much legislative activity on this is-

sue and on the amount of control that schools will retain over the students. *Hazelwood School District v. Kuhlmeier*, 484 U.S. 260 (1988). See Don Corrigan, "Push to Undo Hazelwood Decision," *St. Louis Journalism Review*, February 1992.

10. Donald Rogers, *Banned! Book Censorship in the Schools* (New York: Julian Messner, 1988), p. 101.

11. *Board of Education, Island Trees Union Free School District No. 26 v. Pico*, 457 U.S. 853 (1982).

12. 393 U.S. 97 (1969).

13. Rogers, *Banned!* p. 8.

14. A discussion of this incident appears in Rogers, *Banned!* pp. 130–141.

15. Rogers, *Banned!* p. 18–19.

16. Rogers, *Banned!* p. 20.

17. Rogers, *Banned!* p. 47.

18. Rogers, *Banned!* p. 5.

19. Rogers, *Banned!* p. 7.

20. Lance Morrow, "The Provocative Professor," *Time*, August 26, 1991, p. 19.

21. Reported in the *Cincinnati Post*, March 28, April 7, April 14, 1990, p. 5.

22. Charles-Edward Anderson, "Mapplethorpe Photos on Trial," *ABA Journal*, December 1990, p. 28.

23. For a discussion of this controversy involving Congress and the NEA, see Vince Passaro, "Funds for the Enfeebled," *Harper's*, December 1990, pp. 60–69.

24. Walter Berns, "Saving the NEA." In *1991 First Amendment Law Handbook*, edited by James Swanson (New York: Clark Boardman Callaghan, 1991) p. 312.

25. Passaro, "Funds for the Enfeebled," *Harper's*, p. 63.

26. When chairman John Frohnmayer was replaced by Anne-Imelda Radice, the new chairperson immediately provoked the arts community by making "good on her promise to take control boldly of the government's grant-making process." Kim Masters, "The NEA, Up Against the Cutting Edge," *Washington Post*, May 14, 1992, p. D1.

27. *Rust v. Hill*, 111 U.S. 1759 (1991).

28. The bill would allow so-called indecent programming to be aired only between the hours of midnight and 6 a.m. It also included a requirement that the Corporation for Public Broadcasting (CPB) provide time for public comment on the quality, creativity, diversity, balance, and objectivity of the shows and take those views into account when assessing overall national programming. If CPB decides the programming is one-sided, it must also supply the funds to air opposing views, according to the legislation.

29. *Newsletter on Intellectual Freedom*, September 1990, p. 162.

CHAPTER 9

1. Quoted in Nicols Fox, "Siege of the First Amendment," *Washington Journalism Review*, December 1990, p. 47.

2. Ibid., p. 46.

3. Quoted in David Noble, *Forces of Production: A Social History of Machine Tool Automation* (New York: Alfred A. Knopf, 1984), p. 1.

4. This anxiety is outlined in Mona Harrington, *The Dream of Deliverance in American Politics* (New York: Alfred A. Knopf, 1986).

5. Lee Burress, *Battle of the Books: Literary Censorship in the Public Schools, 1950–1985* (Metuchen, N.J.: Scarecrow Press, 1989), p. 4.

6. Ibid., p. 13.

7. Quoted in Leonard Sussman, *Power, the Press and the Technology of Freedom* (New York: Freedom House, 1989), p. 343.

8. Jason DeParle, "Long Series of Military Decisions Led to Gulf War News Censorship," *New York Times*, May 4, 1991, p. A1.

9. Richard Zoglin, "Just Whose Side Are They On?" *Time*, February 25, 1991, pp. 52–55.

10. See Edward de Grazia and Roger Newman, *Banned Films: Movies, Censors and the First Amendment* (New York: Bowker, 1982), p. 34.

11. See, for instance, Arthur Schlesinger, Jr., *The Disuniting of Society* (New York: W. W. Norton, 1991).

12. Paul Starr, "The Cultural Enemy Within," *The American Prospect* I, no. 4 (Winter 1991): 9.

13. Fox, "Siege of the First Amendment," p. 45.

Suggested Reading

Berman, Paul, ed. *Debating P.C.: The Controversy over Political Correctness on College Campuses*. New York: Laurel Books, 1991.

Bollinger, Lee. *The Tolerant Society: Freedom of Speech and Extremist Speech in America*. New York: Oxford University Press, 1986.

Boyer, Paul S. *Purity in Print: The Vice-Society Movement and Book Censorship in America*. New York: Charles Scribner's Sons, 1968.

Curry, Richard O., ed. *Freedom at Risk: Secrecy, Censorship and Repression in the 1980s*. Philadelphia: Temple University Press, 1988.

DelFattore, Joan. *What Johnny Shouldn't Read: Textbook Censorship in America*. New Haven: Yale University Press, 1992.

Emerson, Thomas I. *Toward a General Theory of the First Amendment: A Unique Examination of the Nature of Freedom of Expression and Its Role in a Democratic Society*. New York: Random House, 1966.

Gardner, Gerald. *The Censorship Papers: Movie Censorship Letters from the Hays Office, 1934 to 1968*. New York: Dodd, Mead, 1987.

Grazia, Edward de, and Roger K. Newman. *Banned Films: Movies, Censors and the First Amendment*. New York: R. R. Bowker, 1982.

Jansen, Sue Curry. *Censorship: The Knot That Binds Power and Knowledge*. New York: Oxford University Press, 1988.

Leff, Leonard J., and Jerold L. Simmons. *The Dame in the Kimono: Hollywood, Censorship and the Production Code from the 1920s to the 1960s*. New York: Grove Weidenfeld, 1990.

Murphy, Paul L. *World War I and the Origins of Civil Liberties in the United States*. New York: W. W. Norton, 1979.

Smolla, Rodney. *Free Speech in an Open Society.* New York: Alfred A. Knopf, 1992.
Woods, L. B. *A Decade of Censorship in America. 1966–1975.* Metuchen, N.J.: Scarecrow Press, 1979.

Index

Time, 66
Tocqueville, Alexis de, 15, 110–11, 118
To Kill a Mockingbird (Lee), 3, 21, 93
Tomorrow's Children, 6
Truman, Harry, 130
Truman Doctrine, 130
Truth: ideological, 55; individual, 39; judicial, 45; objective, 56; pleasant, 44; political, 50, 54; pragmatic view of, 48; rational, 54; scientific, 39; secondary treatment of, 45; social, 39–40, 41–42, 44, 48–49, 50; spiritual, 39; unpleasant, 44
Tufts University, 58
2 Live Crew, 3, 4, 5, 32, 83, 90, 115

Uhl, Wayne, 90
Ulysses (Joyce), 31, 112
Un-Americanism, 73–75, 130, 134
United Nations, 17, 132
Universities: Arizona, 56; Arizona State, 60; California at Berkeley, 60; Connecticut, 59; Dayton, 93; District of Columbia, 101; Michigan, 57, 58, 59; Missouri, 57; Pennsylvania, 58; Seton Hall, 133; Texas, 58; Washington, 58; Yale, 59

United States v. Associated Press, 41
U.S. Commission on Civil Rights, 60

Values Clarification (Simon et al.), 21
Vassar College, 57
Vietnam War, 17, 56, 77, 131
Violence, 90, 103

Warhol, Andy, 92
Warner Brothers Records, 91
Watergate, 53
Westmoreland, General William, 17, 92
Whatmough, Joshua, 93
Where Eagles Dare, 6
White Aryan Resistance, 105
Whitney v. California, 41
Why Americans Hate Politics (Dionne), 35
Wilson, Woodrow, 23
Witchcraft, 108, 133
Wojnarowicz, David, 102
Women in Love (Lawrence), 31
World War I, 17, 20, 29, 114
World War II, 1, 130, 131

Yale University, 59

About the Author

PATRICK GARRY is a Visiting Scholar at Columbia University School of Law and a Fellow at the Freedom Forum Media Studies Center at Columbia University, where he is researching and writing on media and First Amendment topics. He is the author of *An American Vision of a Free Press* (1990) and *Liberalism and American Identity* (1992).